MINDFUL IN 5™

God Lovers' Edition

Discover Your Peaceful Path

Spiwe Jefferson, CMP, JD

Archway Publishing books may be ordered through booksellers or by contacting:

Archway Publishing
1663 Liberty Drive
Bloomington, IN 47403
www.archwaypublishing.com
844-669-3957

ISBN: 978-1-6657-3648-0 (sc)
ISBN: 978-1-6657-5407-1 (hc)
ISBN: 978-1-6657-3649-7 (e)

Library of Congress Control Number: 2023900203

Print information available on the last page.

Archway Publishing rev. date: 12/04/2023

DISCLAIMER

This work consists of fictional characters and composites of some real and fictionalized events. Names, characters, businesses, places, events, locales, and incidents are either the products of the author's imagination or used in a fictitious manner. Any resemblance to actual persons, living or dead, or actual events is purely coincidental.

This publication is based on more than a decade of research, experience, and interviews. It provides practical information related to the subject matter covered. It does not render medical, psychological, legal, or other advice. Consult a qualified professional in the respective field if such guidance is needed.

Although the author has made every effort to ensure that the information in this book was correct at press time, the author does not assume and hereby disclaims any liability to any party for any loss, damage, or disruption caused by errors or omissions, whether such errors or omissions result from negligence, accident, or any other cause.

The information in this book is meant to supplement, not replace, proper mindfulness meditation training. Some practices, like sitting in a particular position for long periods of time or reflecting on events or situations that may invoke stressful or negative emotions, may pose some inherent risk, depending on individual emotional, physical, or other condition. The author advises readers to take full responsibility for their safety and to know their limits. Before practicing the skills described in this book, be sure that you are in sufficient physical shape and that you do not need professional emotional or other assistance. Do not take risks beyond your level of experience, aptitude, training, and comfort level.

CONTENTS

DARK

DAWN

DAY

ACKNOWLEDGMENTS

To Papa, who commissioned this work. Your Little Spirit is ever grateful for all that You put before me.

My profound gratitude to Renee Aikens; Anna Bezzo-Clark; Estrellita Doolin; Renee Clippert; Carol Young; Claryce Burris; Tori Richardson-Hill; Alice Hobbs; my executive coach, Stewart Hirsch. Your invaluable insights and thoughtful input were instrumental in shaping this book, ensuring that it reached its fullest potential.

Thank you, First Lady, Hope Patterson of New Hope Baptist Church in St. Paul. What a delight to engage with you in this important work.

Thank you to my pastor and friend, Troy Dobbs at Grace Church of Eden Prairie. Your feedback, your love of God and dedicated teaching, continually deepen my understanding and fuel my own quest to know God better.

Thank you, PeggyAnne Buckner, for your unwavering commitment to teach us how to rightly divide the Word in spirit and in truth.

Deepest thanks to Jerry W. Blackwell. Your guidance led me to the transformative journey of meditation.

Thank you to the one who mastered himself, Paramahansa Yogananda, and the devotees of Self-Realization Fellowship. Your years of meticulous and heartfelt instruction have been nothing short of a beacon, illuminating my peaceful path. Your dedication and wisdom have been a constant source of inspiration.

To my family, TJ, Bernie, Olivia, Jet, and Jamie, thank you for always being willing to listen, read, provide thoughts, and for your unwavering support.

Thank you to everyone who purchased a copy of the first two books in this series, *Mindful in 5 – Meditations for People With No Time,* and the *Mindful in 5 Journal.* Let's continue to change the world for the better, one mindful person at a time.

WHY I WROTE THIS BOOK

I am surrounded by powerful people: powerhouse professionals, devoted parents, and successful executives. These people look like they have it all. But in quiet moments of intimate conversation, they say things like:

"Why do I still feel like I'm not good enough?"

"I thought achieving this level of success in my career would make me happy."

"Is this all there is?"

We are surrounded by fear, division, and the perception of scarcity. Technology keeps us connected more than ever, yet depression and loneliness are on the rise. And more people seem to have trouble turning off their minds or sleeping. With every complaint I thought, *I have a suggestion for that.*

My Wilderness Journey

Years ago, my life was in turmoil. I was getting divorced, and at stake was everything I had counted on: my marriage, children, home, friends, finances, and future plans. Some psychologists say death and divorce are among the worst experiences we can encounter. My father, who I loved and respected, had a heart attack and passed away three months after my divorce was final. For years I felt adrift in a wilderness with no light on the horizon. How I found my way through that dark and desolate time is reflected in the pages of this book.

My Way Back on the Mindfulness Meditation Path

In 2005 a friend introduced me to meditation. A devoted lover of God, I have long been a student of the Bible. But while Jesus taught us how to pray, and the Bible instructs us to meditate, it provides no step-by-step guide to meditation.

Thus began my journey of meditative learning. I studied formal meditation lessons; read numerous books on mindfulness and meditation; and attended meditation sessions, services, conferences, and retreats. I practiced using various tools and techniques under the guidance of yogis and experts. I became a certified mindfulness practitioner, and because mindfulness meditation is a path and not a destination, I continue to be a student of devotional, self-help, and inspirational books on how to weather life's challenges.

How Mindfulness Changed My Life

I originally embarked on the mindfulness meditation journey on a quest to deepen my relationship with God. By the time the calamities fell, I had progressed on the path to achieving greater stillness in my meditation time. It was during those God-centered meditations that clarity came – to change your life, you must change yourself. Don't waste time trying to change the people around you. Changing yourself empowers you to make different choices and withstand the challenges that come at you – whether relational or situational.

It didn't happen in a day, a week, or a month. But over time, God healed me from the emotional devastation of my personal losses and brought me into a new realm of ever-new joy, love, and peace. Mindfulness meditation accelerated that process and gave birth to a much stronger, calmer, and more centered self. Before, I was a reed tossed about by the winds of emotional and daily upheaval. Now I'm an oak tree, firm and stable on my rock and solid foundation, even when the howling gales of change and calamity arise. It doesn't exempt me from the ups and downs of life, but my faith and trust in that divine relationship is bottomless. It allows me to stand strong through them from an emotional and psychological place of equanimity and power.

What Mindfulness Can Do for You

This power is within you too, and this book will help you unleash it. For God lovers, the power is magnified because you can attach yourself to an endless source far greater than anything you can achieve in your own strength. I wrote this book because I long to share the inner peace and strength I have found to weather life's challenges. Life may not always be easy, but God is with you always. Have faith that He's there even if you don't feel His presence.

Mindfulness meditation will not solve your problems but with consistent practice, your ability to sit with God and cultivate a deep, loving relationship will improve your outlook, attitude, and overall quality of life. It will unlock and unleash your inner strength, allowing you to overcome the challenges of daily life with deeper calm and unflappable focus. The power is within you. Unleash it and tip into it. In the stillness of concentration, you will hear more clearly the still, small voice that is God within you. He won't shout above the din of your restless thoughts, but if you seek Him with a sincere and loving heart, you will find Him. Stay faithful that it will happen even if it takes a while.

Whether you are a novice who has never meditated before, or a seasoned yogi with years of practice, this book provides topics you can use in any season of life. I extend joy and peace to you as you explore your life at a deeper level by walking through the pages of this book.

May you harness the power of mindfulness to live and work to your highest and best purpose each day. Win the game of life no matter what challenges you face.

ABOUT THE GOD LOVERS' EDITION

This edition contains similar reflections to those in the Classic Edition of *Mindful in 5*, but for people who want to focus their reflections on God. In numerous verses (some of which you'll find throughout this book), my life manual, the Holy Bible, exhorts us to meditate. In my experience the most effective way to draw closer to God is through a combination of both prayer and meditation. There are many definitions of meditation, but my favorite came from a friend who said, "Prayer is your opportunity to talk to God; meditation is creating space for God to talk to you."

Who is this God?

We cannot have a solid conversation about God without first level-setting and clarifying of whom we speak.

As someone from a different culture, my own spiritual journey has showed me that the concept of God is not limited to a single people group, religion, or dogma. In my experience, God is much broader and more inclusive than any one specific belief system can capture. He is the creator and ruler of the universe and all that exists within it. He is omniscient, omnipotent, benevolent, and transcendent. And the most amazing part about Him is that He wants a personal relationship with each and every one of us. But He will never force Himself on you. The loving parent that He is, He cares about every joy, heartache, and challenge you experience.

All religions have something to offer. Jesus is my home but there are many sources of teaching and while there are many differences, there are also many areas of spiritual overlap among the religions. I am originally from Zimbabwe, and in my native tongue, Shona, the word for God is Mwari (pronounced mwah-ree), and His son's name is Jesu (pronounced Jeh-soo). I have a friend who did not enjoy a positive earthly paternal relationship. He prefers to refer to God as Divine Mother, a term used by many devotees around the world.

Even in the Christian Bible, the apostle Paul defines God as spirit. "He" is formless. "They" are three in one (the Trinity). Both man and woman were created in "His" image. "He" defines Himself as "I Am", which is Divine Consciousness. Other people think of God as Divine Energy. The point here is that the true essence of God is formless spirit. Assigning a gender is for the ease of reference for a human race that finds it easier to relate to a Divine Being on the basis of gender. Hence, for consistency, I will refer to God in this book as male.

Don't allow dogma and philosophical differences stand between you and your creator.

The life manual I am most intimately familiar with and the guiding principles I follow are rooted in the Bible. For this reason, I have mostly used verses from the Hebrew Bible or Tanakh, which are common to both Jews and Christians. The Indian character, Singita has Hindu roots, so you will notice that most of the chapters that focus on her, begin with quotes from the Bhagavad Gita, her life manual. All the verses and quotes at the beginning of each chapter illustrate important spiritual concepts. I invite you to sit with God and ask Him to illuminate for you how these principles translate in your own life.

Rather than focusing on the specific details of a particular religion, I believe that our ultimate goal should be to build a relationship with God.

This relationship can take many forms, and it is up to you to find and operate from your own spiritual path and craft your own personal relationship with a God ready to speak to you in the language of your heart. By approaching the Divine in this way, with humble desire and openness, you can begin to transcend cultural and religious boundaries, and connect with a higher power that is universal to all people, regardless of their background or beliefs.

The examples and tools in this book provide a vision of what it looks like to weave God into every day through all the ups and downs. He will never force Himself on you. Regardless of what religion or belief system you follow, starting your day by centering your mind on God can have a profound impact on your sense of peace and wellbeing. Pursue Him as a star-struck lover pursues their beloved, and He will answer the call of your heart. Focusing your attention on the Divine can help you feel more centered and grounded throughout the day. It also gives you a deeper sense of who you really are and creates a path for you to transcend the daily issues grounded in ego, attachment to the body, expectation, and materiality, that often cause fear and foster suffering and discord.

By quieting your mind and turning your thoughts towards God, you may find that you are better able to cope with stress and anxiety and approach each day with a greater sense of peace, purpose, and clarity. So, I invite you to start with just five minutes each morning to meditate on God and see how this simple practice can transform your life in powerful ways.

Isn't God Angry and Scary?

Some cultures and religions paint a picture of a vengeful, angry God, who hovers over you waiting to condemn you for screwing up or going astray. This perspective is misguided and mischaracterizes writings from the Bible, the Torah, and other religious texts in a flat, one-dimensional, and erroneous context.

God, the creator of all things, embodies love at His core and longs for a deep and intimate connection with you. It may seem astounding, but the truth remains: the God of the universe desires a personal relationship with you, no matter how insignificant you may feel. His love knows no limits, and in the darkest of seasons, He will seek you out, stand beside you, and carry you through. However, to truly witness His transformative work in your life, a relationship is essential. Unsure of where to start? Dedicate your quiet moments to prayer and meditation, focusing on God. Surrender your life to Him, turn away from wrongdoing, and ask Him to guide you in building a relationship with Him. He will reveal the immeasurable richness that awaits you when He takes the helm of your life. Take this step, and embark on a journey of divine love and fulfillment.

If God Loves Me, Why Does He Let the Dark Season Happen?

This question perplexes many people. Some lose their faith and abandon their relationship with God when life throws them lemons. But it is in the Dark season that we should cling to God most closely. Having lost both my parents, I can attest to the pain of Dark seasons. But even then, I could see God's kindness in how these events occurred. For instance, my dad passed away just four months after my divorce was final. I was already down in the bottom of my Dark season. How much worse would it have been if God had waited for me to do all the hard work of recovering, only to toss me down to the bottom of that well again? Neither of my parents suffered long before they transitioned; a kindness since, emotionally, they would have fared very poorly in a prolonged illness. Separated by continents, it would have been impossible for my sister and me to provide adequate care and to be there had either parent needed long-term care. This logic may sound morbid, but just because we hated the outcome (the departure of our parents) doesn't mean God didn't extend His grace in the process.

In a culture that has become accustomed to the concept of helicopter parents, it can be difficult to fathom a loving God who doesn't rush to cushion every fall or fend off illness, natural disasters and other calamities. We live in a fallen world full of bent and broken people. One of the greatest gifts that God gave us was unfettered and unconditional choice, and the fact is that many of the ills that befall us are born of either our choices or the choices of others. Drunk driving accidents, 9/11, wars, poverty, and even some natural disasters are traceable back to choices made by individuals, businesses, and governments. If you're honest, how many times have you yourself made choices that ran your life off the cliff. Then there you lay, at the bottom of the ravine, yelling and shaking your fist at God as if He put you down there.

The Bible is replete with ordinary people who make bad choices that cost them dearly. For example, Adam and Eve ate the forbidden fruit, costing them their blissful life in the Garden of Eden. David committed murder and adultery, costing him his young son. Most of the residents of Sodom and Gomorrah lived in depravity, causing God to send down angels who destroyed the cities and most of their inhabitants. The original inhabitants of the promised land (the Canaanites, Jebusites, Hittites, and the other "ites") were steeped in idolatry (the worship of inanimate gods), causing God to instruct the Israelites to kill them all and take their land. In Egypt, Pharoah refused to free the enslaved Jewish people, bringing the 10 plagues upon his entire country, one of which was the death of every first-born Egyptian child. Jephthah promised to sacrifice the first thing out of his house if God rendered him victorious in war. It cost him his only teenage daughter. My pastor says the "sacrifice" was not to kill her, but to give her life over to God, meaning she couldn't marry or have children (think, committing your only teenage daughter to become a lifelong nun).

The Bible shows us that bad things happen for many reasons. In the case of Job, God allowed Satan to heap calamities on Job, a righteous man, to prove that man's capacity for love and faith in God can transcend man's own comfort and the blessings God gives him. Interestingly, it also appears that before he lost it all, Job had lived in fear of losing it all.

For the thing which I greatly feared is come upon me, and that which I was afraid of is come unto me.
Job 3:25 New King James Version (NKing James Version)

Would God have chosen him to be this example had Job not been manifesting this fear? The Bible doesn't explain, but I have always thought this twist interesting. Much has been written about the power of personal manifesting, the consistency of universal laws in delivering to us the experiences that we intentionally or unwittingly put out into the world. The Bible says, *Ask, and it will be given to you; seek, and you will find; knock, and it will be opened to you. (Matthew 7:7 New King James Version).* Hence, it lends credence to the notion that sometimes, bad things happen because we unwittingly invite them by ruminating over them and giving energy to them.

There is no written text that I'm aware of where God promises us a trouble-free life. In fact, the Bible expressly assures us that in this life, troubles will come. It provides ample examples of God lovers who were beset with tragedies and trials. So, if you are mad at God for not giving you a cushy life of comfort, abandon the notion! What God does promise, is that through all of it, He will be there helping us and even carrying us when we cannot stand. He encourages us to lean on Him, cast our cares on Him to lighten our burden.

The Lord is for me; I will not be afraid. What can man do to me? The Lord is my helper, Therefore, I will look in triumph on those who hate me.
        Psalm 118:6-7 Holman Christian Standard Bible

HOW TO USE THIS BOOK

The purpose of this book is to help you draw closer to God in your daily practice. Every week's meditation encourages you to invite God into your meditation practice and consult Him, seek His guidance, and share Your life with Him. Start your meditation time with a prayer. It can be as long or as short as you like. Think of it as introducing yourself or greeting someone when you first see them. Then use the topic of the day to focus your thoughts during your five-minute meditation. For extra effectiveness you can journal before or after your five-minute meditation.

If you already view God as a loving and trusted life companion, this book may feel familiar and comforting.

If you have never spoken or thought about God this way, take a risk and step into a new kind of relationship with Him. If this is not the paradigm of God you grew up with, take a risk.

Some people stay stuck in indecision, waiting for God to magically appear and definitively declare the direction they should take. There are times when you might ask God a question and immediately receive a definitive answer, either directly or through people or events He sends into your life to deliver answers. A fundamental tenet behind this book is that while God will help and guide you when He deems it necessary and appropriate (not to be confused with when you think He should show up), your job is not to simply sit there and wait for Him to do things for you. So, seek Him out in your meditation time and take the steps that seem right. He will come alongside you in all the ways He deems fit.

If you don't see evidence of His hand in your life, it may be that you have not yet cultivated the discernment to know when He's talking to you directly or indirectly. Don't get hung up on that. God is not a genie who appears upon the rubbing of a lamp or the recitation of a special incantation. Continue to sincerely practice stillness with pure intention, and sooner or later, you will experience His presence. How will you know? You just will.

Every soul recognizes its creator.

I recommend you read the entire book in sequence at least once. Doing so will acclimate you to the content and allow you to use it as an effective reference based on your own season from day to day. It will also prevent you encountering spoilers in what happens with the four friends who are illustrating the journey. Thereafter, select the season that best suits your current mindset, from the three seasons – Dark, Dawn, and Day. The chapters in these three seasons will take you through 52 weeks, encouraging you to spend five minutes of prayer and meditation per day, five reflections per week.

Regardless of how new or mature you are on the mindfulness meditation path, take a gander through the Practice section. After Practice, three parts follow: Dark, Dawn, and Day. Here we meet four strangers who become friends during a year of attending a support group together. Their journey through the seasons illustrates their individual struggles and how they harness the power of mindfulness to face the ups and downs of each day.

Because it can be challenging to sit still even for five minutes at a time, use the topics to center your thoughts. On any given day, however, feel free to veer off topic and focus on any issue relevant to you in the moment.

Three Seasons

While weather seasons are not the same around the world, every day can be divided into the same three parts: Dark, Dawn, and Day. In this book, each season represents a different time in your life, or simply how you feel from one day to the next.

You may feel that what I am calling "seasons" are out of order; after all, shouldn't they be organized in the same progression as during a regular day—dawn, day, dark? No. The order is intentional. Most people become reflective and seek answers when facing difficulties, hence the book begins with dark. Once you make it through this season, you then encounter dawn, a season of new possibilities that carries you into the bright sun of day.

Pegin by reading the "Practice" chapters. Journey into mindfulness meditation with two friends, Akar and Chantelle. Akar struggles with many challenges you might face in getting started on your mindfulness meditation journey. Chantelle, a mindful ninja, encourages him and provides suggestions to help Akar troubleshoot his practice. Use Chantelle's example and guidance to show you what life can look like when you're on your mindfulness game.

Dark: In this season you encounter the worst emotional and psychological pain of your life. It could be triggered by a job loss, someone's death, a significant breakup, a pandemic, a terrible medical diagnosis, or physical or psychological trauma. You may question yourself, your life, and everything you thought was true. This is when it is most critical to take time and set your intentions and mental framework each day. Create space for God to carry you through.

Dawn: This is a season of new beginnings—a move to a new place, the birth of a child, a new marriage or relationship, a new job, or simply the joy of a new day. You see great possibilities ahead and want to take full

advantage of the best this time has to offer. Because life is looking up, you may want to sprint headlong into your future. But allowing God to guide you brings wisdom that will elevate you even more.

Day: You are moving through your happy, routine life. The sun is shining; all is well, maybe even a bit boring. Happiness and even joy may come easily, and people might mistake you for someone who lives a

charmed life with no problems. In this season more than any other, you have the capacity to devote emotional energy to your walk with God because you're not spending it battling difficulties. In this life, you *will* have troubles. Darkness comes to all based on your type of Dark season.

God-centered meditation during your Day season can prolong your season of Day and will reduce the severity of the impact of the Dark season when it arrives.

Difference Between Prayer and Meditation

You will see references to both these terms in this book. You might be wondering about the difference.

> *Prayer is talking to God. God-centered meditation involves creating space for God to talk to you.*

Prayer is a deeply personal and sacred practice, and there is no singular correct way to approach it. It is a heartfelt connection between you and the Divine, where you can express your innermost thoughts, fear, pain, desires, and gratitude. In the Christian Bible, Jesus gave His disciples a prayer they could recite. Monks, pastors, priests, gurus, imams, and spiritual leaders the world over share scripted and spontaneous words in prayer.

Whether it takes the form of scripted words or an unfiltered outpouring of emotions, the essence lies in the intention behind it. The key is to approach prayer with reverence and humility, acknowledging our place in the vastness of the universe and seeking guidance or solace. In this profound act, we find solace, strength, and a sense of unity with something greater than ourselves. The characters in this book embrace the diversity of prayer in their myriad situations, knowing that each sincere offering is valuable and meaningful in its own unique way.

God wants to have a relationship with you. If you are a loving parent, or if you have one in your life, it is easier to understand the concept of a parent with boundless love who wants to have a fulsome relationship with his or her child. Why? Because God is your parent. He is the ultimate life companion who can help – and even carry you – through all of life's hills and valleys. He can celebrate all triumphs great and small, He can most efficiently guide you through your season of Dark, show you how to prolong your stay in the seasons of Dawn and Day. But most of all, walking with Him can produce the most fulfilling relationship you will ever experience.

God-centered meditation encourages you to do much more than show up at God's doorstep with demands and complaints. It invites you to hang out and just be present with your Creator as you would spend time with your best friend. It invites you to listen for His voice and engage in dialogue. He may speak to you directly, or He may send people and signs to answer questions, provide direction, and confirm. He may point you to passages in the Bible or elsewhere for answers. After all, He has the world and everything in it, at His disposal to talk back to you. Meditation allows you to declutter your mind, making it easier to hear His voice and receive His insights. Show up in the spirit of love and trust. He will always be there, even if you can't sense it.

Be Kind to Yourself

As you begin using this guide, you might find yourself jumping between the seasons. The primary goal is for you to use the season that meets you where you are at any given moment. And since you can jump around the book, use the graphic images at the top of each page along with the chapter numbers as guideposts for where you are in a particular season.

It's okay if it takes you months or even years to move past a particular chapter. Issues like acknowledging pain, letting go, and forgiveness can take years to address fully. Give yourself permission to go at your own pace.

God won't be mad at you if you don't talk to Him for a while. But He'll delight in you when you do.

Don't beat yourself up if your practice ebbs and flows. That's normal. Just keep coming back to it whenever you can.

How to Invite God Into Your Life

You don't have to be ready to commit your life to God to gain valuable insights and learn from this book. However, if you are ready to invite God into your life as you embark on this meditative journey, you can do so by reciting a prayer of invitation, such as:

Dear God,

I open my heart to invite You into my life. I embrace Your love, forgiveness, and transformative power. Today, I choose to turn from my wrong ways of living and follow Your path of righteousness. I release the burdens that weigh me down and find solace in Your presence. Heal my wounds, restore my soul, and guide me to a life filled with purpose and joy. I surrender to Your loving embrace, experiencing the freedom and peace that come from walking with You. Thank You for Your abundant grace. Amen.

P

PRACTICE

Reflections to Get You Going

Chantelle has been meditating for years, and Akar begins because he wants the peace she has. Akar's is not a smooth journey. He doesn't know where to practice, how to sit, or what to think about. Meanwhile, life and work continue to present challenges, and he gets discouraged. Many of us experience Akar's struggles along the path to mindful peace. Be encouraged. Keep learning. Keep moving toward your higher self. Stay on the path!

CHAPTER 1

WHY MEDITATION?

*My mouth speaks wisdom; my heart's meditation brings
understanding.*

Psalms 49:3 Holman Christian Standard Bible

"How'd you do it?" Akar Khouri, global vice president of sales, asked
the chief legal officer at lunch. They sat under an orange umbrella at
a picnic table in a manicured courtyard at Sunderland Medical, Inc.
"Gottfried is a lunatic. You're a military wife juggling three kids. How
are you so calm?"

Chantelle Dubois smiled sadly. Just then, a man broke from a tour
of new employees and hurried over. "Hey, aren't you Vivek Murthy, the
former US surgeon general?" he demanded in excitement.

"No!" Akar snapped. "Can't you tell the difference between an Indian and an Egyptian?" The man retreated apologetically.

Chantelle's cheek dimpled. Although Akar was Egyptian and Dr. Murthy was of Indian descent, and their complexions were quite different, Akar did resemble the former surgeon general. His lithe frame, sloped shoulders, regal nose, and distinguished salt-and-pepper hair were strikingly similar. She replied, "I meditate for thirty minutes twice a day."

"And?" Akar asked, raking agitated fingers through his hair.

"That's it. My peace comes from God within."

Akar scowled. The French woman continued in her pleasant, accented lilt, "I observe my thoughts and emotions. God guides and holds me together regardless of events." Chantelle thought about Dale Anderson, her husband, waking up screaming in the middle of the night. She brought herself back to the present.

"I don't have an hour for daily meditation." Akar sighed. "I'm a sales guy. Go, go, go is my mantra."

Five minutes a day can keep the blues at bay. Just start. It adds up.

The Takeaway

Like Akar, many people would like the benefits and results of mindfulness meditation but doubt they have time. You invested time in this book, so you obviously care about your wellness. If you don't have time, just start with five minutes each morning. You can do it.

My Journal Reflections

Invite God into your practice and start with a prayer, then spend at least five minutes in silent meditation first thing each morning on one of the topics below. You can journal your insights before or after your five-minute meditation for deeper clarity. It will feel like a long time when you start. But stick with it and it will get easier.

Day 1.   For the next five minutes, imagine how life would be different if you could consistently lean on God to better weather life's challenges. Visualize the peace and joy that could be yours each day.

Day 2.   Today, reflect on how your life could be different with consistent use of mindfulness meditation. How do you think this practice can help you?

Day 3.   For the next five minutes, consider your personal habits and circadian rhythms. Are you a morning or night person? Based on those considerations, what is your optimal time of day to meditate and why? If you are uncertain, ask God to illuminate what your best meditation habits look like.

Day 4.   In your meditation time today, accept that you might be able to influence and persuade, but generally, you can't control other people. Ask God to give you comfort with this idea, and then focus your meditation on the things that you *can* control. Accepting this distinction will increase your peace and reduce frustration and stress.

Day 5.   In today's meditation, ask God to help you visualize what your life and relationships will look like going forward if you stop trying to control people and things that you can't. Perhaps focus on a specific person or situation that is particularly significant to you.

CHAPTER 2
DEBUNKING THE MYTHS

May the words of my mouth and the meditation of my heart
be acceptable to You, Lord, my rock and my Redeemer.
Psalms 19:14 Holman Christian Standard Bible

"Isn't mindfulness meditation some weird Eastern mystic crap?"
Akar demanded. His deep brown eyes widened in horror as he heard
himself.

Chantelle's lustrous auburn hair was piled high on her head, and she
tucked a stray curl behind her ear as she began. "Many world religions
share the same fundamental truths about how to live harmoniously
and how to love yourself and others," she said. She explained that while
the cultivation of mindfulness stemmed from Buddhist practices, most

religions—including Hinduism, Islam, and Christianity—advocated prayer and meditation as core practices.

Akar looked skeptical. "Well, I'm a Christian," he said, looking doubtful.

"Then go find your Bible and count how many times it tells you to meditate on the word."

"So, what do I do? Just sit there and empty my mind?" Akar snorted.

"No, that's a myth. You cultivate internal stillness so you can better hear God's voice, feel His presence, and see His hand moving in your life. Attach to God, focus on His word, transform more into His character."

Akar was still not convinced. "So, if I sit and think positive thoughts, my problems will go away?"

Chantelle's laugh was deep and sonorous. "The world won't stop delivering problems to your doorstep. But you will get much better at handling them from a place of calm, personal power and emotional equilibrium," she explained. "God didn't say you wouldn't have trouble in life. What He did say is not to fear because He will be with you always."

The Takeaway

There are many myths about meditation. It's not a silver bullet or quick fix just as having a relationship with God is not an antidote to encountering painful life experience. Meditation is a recognized discipline deeply rooted in the Bible and other religious practices.

God-centered meditation is not about changing others or your environment; it's about transforming your mind so you can hear God more clearly and see the world more through God's eyes.

This journey is not about controlling your terrible boss, that cantankerous spouse, or your badly behaved kids. It's about equipping you with tools and paradigms that will make you better at handling them.

My Journal Reflections

Think about things that turn your mind to God. Pray by speaking to God in the language of your heart. Then set your alarm for five minutes and meditate on a topic below for five minutes. You can journal before or after your five minutes of prayer and meditation for deeper clarity. It will feel like a long time when you start. But stick with it and it will get easier.

Day 1. You cannot address what you don't acknowledge. So spend five minutes today confronting objections you have to practicing mindfulness meditation. Where did this objection come from, and how can you use what you are learning to overcome those objections?

Day 2. Sometimes our ideas about mindfulness and meditation are based on what other people tell us. Today, ask God to open your spiritual eyes to the sources of your biases against mindfulness meditation, especially if they come from others. Are there ways you can accept other people as they are but still be confident and steadfast enough to craft your own beliefs?

Day 3. Today, spend some time reviewing your go-to religious text and look at a few of its references to meditation. Spend time reflecting on how it instructs you to use meditation and practice following those instructions. Ask God to show you how and trust your intuition as your understanding expands.

Day 4.   Today, go within and share with God the things you hope to gain from your mindfulness meditation practice. Then sit quietly and wait to see if there are other insights that come to you.

Day 5.   Today, go within and ask God to show you how your life can be different with your consistent commitment to harness the power of mindfulness meditation. Do you see yourself being calmer? More peaceful? Clear about your life and purpose? What else?

CHAPTER 3
DOES IT REALLY WORK?

Keep this Book of the Law always on your lips; meditate on it day and night, so that you may be careful to do everything written in it. Then you will be prosperous and successful.

Joshua 1:8 New International Version

"Does this stuff really work, Chantelle?" Akar asked. Today they had lunch by a fountain on Sunderland's campus. The scent of Chantelle's lavender shampoo and the sound of cascading water made Akar feel like he was on vacation.

With a dainty flick of her wrist, Chantelle brushed away sandwich crumbs from the multicolored scarf she wore over her crisp white shirt and navy-blue skirt. She told him about Jon Kabat-Zinn, a renowned professor who founded the Stress Reduction Clinic at the University of Massachusetts Medical Center. "His research demonstrated that mindfulness improves both physical and mental health. It helps relieve stress, treats heart disease, improves sleep, increases self-esteem, and increases one's capacity to deal with difficult life events."

Akar's thick brows rose.

Chantelle continued, "At Harvard Medical School, a neuroscientist and assistant professor of psychology, Dr. Sara Lazar, was the first to document positive changes in brain regions connected to memory, the sense of self, and the regulation of emotions because of mindfulness meditation. Many prestigious universities and Fortune 500 companies, like Apple, Nike, Google, and even the US Army, have incorporated mindfulness meditation into their health and wellness programs." Chantelle cocked her head and regarded Akar, her kind eyes searching his face. "Centering your meditation on God will help you realize who you truly are, which is much more than this…" Her hand swept over him.

Be still and know that I am God.
Psalm 46:10 New King James Version

The Takeaway

Chantelle grazed the tip of the iceberg. There is a growing volume of empirical scientific data demonstrating emotional, physiological, and psychological benefits of mindfulness meditation in people who practice it consistently. Meditation can provide great depth to your God-centered walk. Being still and making time to hear God's voice is the very best guide to your life. As one who has pursued the mindfulness meditation path for more than seventeen years of the time of writing this book, I can attest to its effectiveness in helping me hear God's voice more frequently and clearly, alleviating stress and increasing my capacity to better navigate difficult times from a place of calm. This peace can be yours too. Keep reading.

My Journal Reflections

Spend at least five minutes in silent meditation first thing each morning, centering yourself and setting your intentions for the day. Set your alarm for five minutes. You can journal after your five minutes of reflection. It will feel like a long time when you start. But stick with it, and it will get easier.

Day 1.   Today, ask God to help you spend the next five minutes just trying to focus on Him and see how that goes. Repeat a simple phrase like "Lord, I love you," and go deeper into the meaning of what that means and what that looks like.

Day 2.   Many people are surrounded by the noise of daily life. Today, silence the rings, dings, chimes, and practice your meditation at a time and in a place where you can have complete silence. It might feel uncomfortable but ask God to show you how to embrace silence in your meditation practice. If your mind wanders, just bring it gently back to enjoy the silence.

Day 3.   Today, ask God to help you visualize clearly what it would look like to be at your best for a particular portion of your upcoming day.

Day 4.   Based on what you have learned so far, today visualize yourself taking different actions that incorporate mindfulness meditation into your daily life. For instance, you can see yourself taking a five-minute break during the day to reset your intentions to move with a calm and positive demeanor. Or you can see yourself pausing before responding in a conversation to be thoughtful.

Day 5.   Today, think about what kind of support you need to keep your God-centered meditation practice going. How can God help you? Ask Him. What actions can you take to keep your habit going? Wake up a little earlier? Take five minutes to meditate before bed time? What else? The more clearly you can visualize those actions you need to take, the more likely you will take the actions you commit to.

CHAPTER 4

WHEN YOU HAVE
NO TIME

He went out to the field one evening to meditate, and as
he looked up, he saw camels approaching.

Genesis 24:63 New International Version

"Did you do it?" Chantelle asked Akar the next day.

Akar's dark eyes bounced around the room, and his bronze face blushed. A sheepish look crept across his handsome face. When her wise gaze finally captured his eyes, he blurted out the truth. "I can't take time for mindfulness. My wife insists on a nightly family dinner, the kids get up early, and I must help prepare them for school in the morning."

Chantelle's deep blue eyes twinkled; her sage smile unfaltering. She knew his wife well, Zahra the spitfire.

He threw up his hands. "How can I take time for mindfulness when I never have time for me?"

The Takeaway

Many share Akar's problem. Daily activities crowd our lives, leaving little to no room for the Divine. But taking time to connect with the Divine will improve your ability to handle everything else. It also allows you to set your intentions and recenter yourself to your spiritual anchor when unexpected challenges arise.

God created the world in six days. On the seventh day, even He rested.

Give yourself the luxury of time. Maybe making time means being disciplined enough to wake up at least five minutes earlier every day so you create time to hang out with God and have him center you for the day. Maybe that means taking time before bed to head for your mindfulness space. It could mean forcing yourself to take a break and not spend your entire lunch hour working at your desk.

Maybe it means going to hide in your mindfulness space for five minutes when the family thinks you are in the bathroom.

Visualize how peaceful and less alone you will feel when you can consistently experience God's presence in your life. Visualize how much better and more effective you will be as a friend, employee, spouse, partner, or parent if you give yourself this time. You are worth it.

My Journal Reflections

Invite God into your practice and spend at least five minutes in silent meditation first thing each morning centering yourself and setting your intentions for the day. Then set your alarm for five minutes and meditate on a topic below for five minutes. You can journal before or after your five minutes of prayer and meditation for deeper clarity. It will feel like a long time when you start. But stick with it and it will get easier.

Day 1.   Ask God to show you how to make space for yourself each day this week and visualize yourself taking steps that will give you five minutes of time daily.

Day 2.   If you sometimes feel guilty taking time for yourself, invite God to sit with you as you explore the reasons for your feelings of guilt. In your meditation, unpack the reasons for your guilt and ask God to help you see the truth of your situation.

Day 3.   What preparations can you make each day to increase the likelihood that you will take five minutes to meditate daily? Wake up earlier? Set out a particular chair or blanket to sit on or cover yourself? Put this book in a particular location? Visualize yourself taking the necessary action to prepare for your five-minute mindfulness reflection.

Day 4.   Today, ask God to help you develop a short phrase you can recite daily to give yourself permission to take five minutes for meditation. Identify that phrase in your mind. Repeat it, and meditate with increasing concentration on what it means to you.

Day 5.   Mindfulness involves being present in the moment without judgment or overwhelm. Self-judgment can be a hindrance to developing a successful meditation practice. If you miss a day (and you will!), ask God to help you develop a short phrase you can recite daily to forgive yourself and get back on track without feeling like you have fallen short. It can be as simple as, *I forgive myself for missing a day,* or *It's okay, I'll just come back to my practice.* In today's five-minute meditation, memorize that phrase and commit to use it and believe it.

P

CHAPTER 5

MINDFULNESS MEDITATION DEFINED

My mouth speaks wisdom; my heart's meditation brings understanding.
Psalm 49:3 Holman Christian Standard Bible

Chantelle's slingback kitten heels clipped in short crisp steps as Akar loped along, hands in the pockets of his suit pants. "What is meditation really?"

Chantelle thought a moment. Then she explained, "Meditation is about so much more than separating yourself from worldly thoughts and feelings to connect with your inner consciousness. It's applying your power of concentration in a disciplined way to go within and connect with God. Contact God and let Him channel all His positive attributes through you."

16

"And what is mindfulness?" Akar asked.

"Mindfulness is the ability to be fully present in the moment without being overly reactive or overwhelmed by what's happening. You calmly acknowledge your thoughts and feelings without judgment. If you get into the habit of living in the present, you eliminate worrying about the future or trying to revise the past."

"So should I pretend the past didn't happen and I have no future?" Akar smirked.

Chantelle was patient with her friend, whose slender frame coiled with nervous energy. "No, Akar. Mindfulness is not about ignoring the past or the future. You can acknowledge the past calmly and without judgment. You can forgive yourself for whatever happened and take actions today that will achieve your desired goals for the future. But you can do it without the needless mind-racing anxiety that yields no positive outcomes."

Akar's thick brows threatened to meet above his regal nose. "And you think this stuff really works?"

"God designed it, science proves it. Do the research." Chantelle's merry eyes sparkling, she added, "Besides, which of us has been upset by Gottfried the last two days?"

You need not be led around by your and others' emotions.

The Takeaway

Chantelle understands that meditation is not about doing but about being, being calm in the presence of upheaval, being confident in who you are as a person God created with intention and purpose.

If you are a committed doer like many people and need something to do, create a list of your mindfulness activities each day.

My Journal Reflections

This week, add mindfulness to your practice. Start the day by meditating for five minutes after starting with a prayer. Remember, starting with just five minutes of God-centered mindfulness meditation can deepen your spiritual journey and strengthen your connection with the Divine. Give yourself the gift of these moments by taking five-minute pauses later during the day.

Day 1.   Close your eyes, take a deep breath, and imagine yourself in the presence of God's loving embrace. Spend five minutes visualizing this sacred connection and feel His peace envelop you. How does it feel?

Day 2.   Take a break from the activity of your day. Close your eyes and spend five minutes focusing on God's presence within you. With each inhale and exhale, let go of worldly worries and invite His divine calm into your being.

Day 3.   Set aside just five minutes to practice mindful prayer. Visualize yourself in conversation with God, fully present and attentive to His gentle guidance. Embrace the power of His divine wisdom and grace. Speak to Him in the language of your heart.

Day 4.   Today, take five minutes to practice gratitude in the presence of God. Close your eyes and visualize moments, blessings, and answered prayers that you're grateful for. Let this gratitude fill your heart and deepen your connection with Him.

Day 5.   Inhale God's love, exhale worldly distractions. Take five minutes to meditate and visualize yourself surrendering any burdens or worries to God's loving care. Fill your mind with His truth, peace, and joy, allowing His presence to illuminate your path.

CHAPTER 6

MINDFULNESS VS. MEDITATION

> *How happy is the man who does not follow the advice of the wicked or take the path of sinners or join a group of mockers! Instead, his delight is in the Lord's instruction, and he meditates on it day and night.*
>
> *Psalm 1:1-2 Holman Christian Standard Bible*

"I'm talking to you. What are you doing?" Chantelle had held up her hand to pause him while she closed her eyes and chewed, and Akar was irritated.

Opening her eyes, she said, "I thanked God for this food before we started eating and now, I'm savoring." Akar stared. "I thought you wanted to practice mindfulness. Why aren't you savoring?"

Akar was confused. "I am. I am doing that sitting thing you told me to do daily."

Chantelle laughed. "You are meditating for five minutes each morning, Akar. But you can practice mindfulness all day."

"Well, how about you mindfully mind what I'm saying?" He grumbled.

The Takeaway

To avoid Akar's confusion, it's helpful to understand the difference between mindfulness and meditation. Meditation is a practice that enables you to detach from worldly thoughts and emotions, allowing you to connect deeply with your inner consciousness. You can use one or more meditative techniques to discipline the mind and increase mental clarity and emotional stability. Creating quiet space in your inner sanctum in the morning allows God to be experienced more clearly.

Although some use mindfulness as a form of meditation, it doesn't require closed eyes or a quiet space. Its goal is to achieve focused presence now without judgment. Carrying that keen sense of awareness throughout your day increases your ability to notice God's hand in your life. Mindfulness can look like:

- Responding with God-like compassion even in the face of abject hostility.
- Being fully focused on a conversation without your mind wandering, eyes tracking other people going by, or planning what to say next.
- Going within and rebooting even when you are engaged in activity.

Begin or end each day by sitting in meditation for five minutes. Then use mindfulness to be fully present in each moment during the remainder of the day.

My Journal Reflections

In the previous chapter, you practiced meditation. Now, practice mindfulness. Remember, dedicating just five minutes to your practice can help bring clarity, peace, and a deeper connection with the Divine. Embrace these moments each day and let God's presence transform your life.

Day 1. Even as you are going about your day, take a moment to center your heart and mind on God's presence. Act with deliberation and intention. Narrow your attention to what you are doing. Invite God to be present with you, allowing His peace to wash over you.

Day 2. Pick up a religious text and reflect on a Scripture passage that speaks to you. Set aside five minutes to reflect on its meaning, allowing God's word to guide your thoughts and shape your perspective.

Day 3. As you go about your day, take five minutes visualizing God's divine light surrounding you, filling you with His wisdom, strength, and peace.

Day 4. In the middle of your activity, take a deep breath and exhale any worries or distractions. Pay close attention to what you are doing. Send up a quick prayer, either thanking God for the opportunity to do what you're doing or inviting God to be present with you. Listen for His gentle voice and feel His loving presence with you.

Day 5.   Choose a God-centered affirmation or mantra. Repeat it silently or aloud for five minutes, allowing its truth to resonate within you. Let the words deepen your trust in God and strengthen your faith.

CHAPTER 7
WHERE TO PRACTICE

But the Lord is in His holy temple; let everyone on earth be
silent in His presence.
Habakkuk 2:20 Holman Christian Standard Bible

Akar watched Chantelle in meetings and in interactions with coworkers. He wanted that same peace and focus. As Sunderland Medical's chief legal officer and one of Gottfried's direct reports, Chantelle was often lumped in with the rest of his team when he raged over the company's performance. Yet, she was unflappable. She sat with her back ramrod straight, sculpted ankles crossed, and chubby fingers gracefully steepled. She spoke her truth gently and with respect, yet with a command that made it clear she knew what she was doing. She even seemed to calm

Gottfried. Stepping out of these meetings, her twinkling eyes and winking dimples were contagiously cheerful. Akar wanted that peace and perpetual optimism.

The first night Akar tried meditating, he sat up in bed. But soon he fell asleep. The next morning, he sat on the couch in the living room, but his son and daughter bounded over to play. The next day, he sat on the toilet, but that felt too weird. And his wife, Zahra, fussed at him for hogging the loo. The next day he sat next to the garage door, but something about the feng shui of sitting by the most trafficked door in the house threw off his energy. He muttered a frustrated prayer, "God, where should I do this?"

"I want a meditation space too," Zahra said. "Why don't we convert the extra bedroom?" The light bulb went on. Ornate Persian tapestries, candles, an altar, cushions, calming pictures. This was the space. It wasn't lost on Akar that the answer to his prayer only came after he asked God for help.

The Takeaway

Like Akar, you may have to try different places to find your ideal meditation spot. It could be a corner, a closet, or an entire room. It doesn't have to be grand. The best space is one that is personal, private, and allows you to show up daily promoting a sense of peace and intimacy with God. You can include art, decorations, instruments, reading materials, or other items that support your practice. Create the space that's right for you.

Always return to that space because over time, your body will become conditioned to calm down when you enter your meditation space. As your practice gains momentum, positive vibrations of love and comfort may germinate in your meditation space.

My Journal Reflections

God delights in your company the way a loving parent enjoys spending time with their children. Don't call on Him only when you need something or when you want to complain. Show up just to spend time with Him and hang out. Our earthly relationships help us understand how to build a relationship with the Divine. Spending positive quality time is a necessary part of any healthy relationship. Start each meditation period by taking a few deep breaths, saying a prayer, then taking five minutes to meditate on the topics below.

Day 1. Take a few deep breaths and relax your body. Imagine yourself in a quiet, cozy room with soft lighting. As you settle into this mental space, envision various spots within your home where you could comfortably meditate. Explore different corners, cushions, chairs, or even a dedicated meditation nook. Notice how each option resonates with you and invite God to guide you towards the spot that feels just right.

Day 2. Close your eyes and take a moment to center yourself. As you breathe deeply, reflect on your decision to find the perfect spot to meditate in your home, affirming its significance in your spiritual journey. Invite God's presence into your heart and trust the wisdom that arises within you and embrace the assurance that you are guided towards the right spot for your sacred practice.

Day 3. Today, sit quietly and reflect on the various places you've encountered throughout your life that have evoked a sense of tranquility within you. Visualize these places one by one, whether it's a favorite park, a secluded spot in your backyard, or a peaceful sanctuary you've visited. As you recall each location, pay attention to the emotions and sensations that arise. Did you feel God's love in any of those spaces? Let these memories guide you towards discovering the perfect spot to meditate, one that holds a deep sense of peace and resonance with your being.

Day 4.   Even if you are not in an ideal spot, you can find peace by going within. Today, close your eyes and envision yourself surrounded by serene natural surroundings. Ask God to help you explore different landscapes, such as a tranquil forest, a serene beach, or a peaceful mountaintop. Let your mind wander and guide you to the perfect spot to meditate. What does it look like? How does it make you feel? Embrace the imagery and allow it to lead you to your ideal meditation spot.

Day 5.   You picked the "home" spot, where you will return to practice mindfulness meditation when you start your day. Today, start by taking a few deep breaths, then sit in that spot for five minutes and see how It feels.

CHAPTER 8

USE FEETS TO MEDITATE

But whose delight is in the law of the Lord, and who meditates on [H]is law day and night. That person is like a tree planted by streams of water, which yields its fruit in season and whose leaf does not wither—whatever they do prospers.

Psalm 1:2-3 New International Version

Decorating the room took some negotiations with the ever-opinionated Zahra, but they finally finished. Akar next considered how to get his meditation on. He laid on a cushion but kept falling asleep. He sat cross-legged on the floor, but his flat butt provided no cushion. He tried a lotus pose he often saw on TV, but that was too difficult. Finally, he sat in a chair. He asked God about it, "Is this an acceptable way to sit?"

Use FEETS

Akar's confusion is understandable since there is no one right way to meditate. But here's a way to start. Start by meditating for five minutes each time. Consistency is more important than length of time. Just get into the habit. An easy mnemonic for the key components of the *Mindful in 5* approach to meditation is FEETS.

1. **F**ind your meditation spot. Use the same place consistently.
2. **E**rgonomic – sit correctly, with spine straight and body relaxed. If you are in a chair, your thighs and feet should be parallel to the floor, with your calves at 90-degree angles to your thighs. If you are on the floor, use a meditation cushion if necessary to help you keep your spine straight without straining.
3. **E**yes – close them to reduce distraction. If you need something to focus on, with your eyes closed, concentrate on the point between your eyebrows, known by some as the center of concentration.
4. **T**opic - visualize a topic from your *Mindful in 5* book, or a topic that speaks to you based on where you are in the moment. Cultivate the practice of speaking to God in the language of your heart. Don't just come to Him when you need something. Notice that while Akar takes time for formal meditation and prayer, some of his prayers sound more like conversations with God. Akar consults God even in everyday things. Treat God like your friends and loved ones on earth; show up with nothing more than a desire to spend quality time with Him. Unlike the way you treat your friends, however, always treat Him with reverence. Your thoughts will wander but this will improve with practice. Never judge or condemn yourself for your wandering mind. Just guide it gently back.

5. **Stillness** – be still and breathe. If you have a hard time settling down, just tell yourself there is nowhere to be, nothing to do, there is only now. In this moment, everything else can wait.

When you're done, slowly open your eyes. Notice how you feel right now. Set your intention; decide how you want to move through this day or the next. Regardless of how the day unfolds, you have the absolute power to choose how *you* will be in it and engage with what comes.

Repeat this meditation practice daily. Throughout your day, take mindful breaks to check in with God. See him in your surroundings, consult him or chat with him as you carry out your tasks. Reflect on how you are feeling, and what's happening in your life without judging it or being overly reactive to it. Remember and reset your intentions for the day as often as you need to.

My Journal Reflections

Invite God into your practice and ask Him to calm your heart and mind so you can get the most out of your five-minute meditation time. Invite Him to journey with you throughout the day and face with you whatever the day brings. Doing this consistently will also increase your consciousness of His divine presence and help you be more attuned to how God moves in your life.

Day 1.   Find a comfortable seated position, aligning your body in correct ergonomic posture. Take a moment to acknowledge God's presence within you, recognizing that your body is a temple of His Spirit. Breathe in His love and exhale any tension or stress, allowing His peace to fill you completely. For today's meditation, work on relaxing the rest of your body while you maintain just enough tension in your spine to keep it straight.

Day 2. Today, as you focus on maintaining correct posture during your meditation, reflect on the divine design of your body. Each vertebra, muscle, and joint intricately crafted by God's wisdom. Offer a prayer of gratitude for the gift of your physical vessel, recognizing that it is through this body that you can serve and glorify Him.

Day 3. Today during your meditation, with each breath, visualize God's grace flowing through your upright spine, bringing alignment and balance not only to your physical body but also to your spiritual being. Allow His divine energy to permeate every cell, revitalizing and renewing you from the inside out.

Day 4. As you gently adjust your posture, imagine that you are aligning yourself with God's perfect will. Just as you seek to find the optimal position for your body's well-being, strive to align your thoughts, actions, and intentions with His divine guidance. Surrender any misalignment or distractions and ask for His guidance in all aspects of your life.

Day 5. Throughout your practice, invite God's presence to inhabit every aspect of your posture and body. With each breath, imagine that His love and grace are filling you, radiating outwards to touch those around you. Pray for His strength and wisdom to maintain an upright posture not just physically, but spiritually, embodying His love and truth in all that you do.

CHAPTER 9

PRACTICE THE
SELF-EMBRACE

---

*The Lord God caused to grow out of the ground every tree
pleasing in appearance and good for food, including the tree
of life in the middle of the garden, as well as the tree of the
knowledge of good and evil.*

Genesis 2:9 Holman Christian Standard Bible

"The company spent $11 million developing this medical device. We've made promises to investors. The product must launch." The senior marketer, who was chairing the meeting, looked around in defiance.

A junior engineer piped up, "The device has a 25 percent failure rate. We can't kill 25 percent of our customers." Battle lines drawn; a fight erupted among the twenty-five employees in the meeting. Akar said nothing as the meeting devolved into a shouting match. Finally, he looked across the massive conference room table for Chantelle's reaction.

To his surprise, she was a statue, eyes closed, hands grasping her elbows as if holding herself together. Then she opened her eyes and stood to her full five-foot two inches, piled braided hair adding a foot. Her appearance shimmered in the table's glass surface. She commanded an immediate hush. "Stop talking," she demanded in her strong sonorous voice. "First, this conversation goes no further." She looked at the employees with pens poised over notebooks. "Close those," she commanded. Then she began to speak.

The Takeaway

Perhaps, next to the gift of life, God's greatest gift to human beings was the gift of free will. So great because even when he granted it, he knew of all the depravity we would conceive with it. And yet he gave us the gift anyway. Many parents spend a lot of time curtailing (or trying to curtail) the choices of their children. Managers spend a lot of time trying to control the choices and behaviors of employees. In every aspect of life people try to influence each other to conform to our efforts to control. But yet God gave us this gift without reservation.

In every event and interaction lies a choice, the choice of how we respond. There are always at least two options. The power to choose is yours. And how you use that power defines your growth and freedom.

How to Self-Embrace

Chantelle was practicing the self-embrace. The self-embrace can increase levels of the hormone oxytocin, which can decrease blood pressure, stress, and reduce your heart rate.

When you feel stressed, practice this simple but powerful technique. Close your eyes. Keep your head up or drop it to your chest. Hug yourself. For extra benefit, add a small smile by slightly upturning the corners of your lips. This invokes the theory of facial feedback hypothesis, which - studies have shown – triggers positive emotions in the brain. You can visualize God holding you in his arms or just focus on your breathing. Disconnect from everything to go within and find your peace. You can revisit the day's *Mindful in 5* reflection or consult God on what to do or say next. You can set a timer, or just embrace yourself until you're ready to resume your activities.

My Journal Reflections

Invite God into your practice and spend at least five minutes in silent meditation first thing each morning centering yourself and setting your intentions for the day. Begin with a prayer and a few deep breaths. Then set your alarm for five minutes and meditate on a topic below for five minutes. You can journal before or after your five minutes of prayer and meditation for deeper clarity. Five minutes will feel like a long time when you start. But stick with it and it will get easier.

Day 1.   For the next five minutes, practice the self-embrace. What's easy about it? What is challenging? How can you incorporate it into your day?

Day 2.   Close your eyes and breathe deeply. Reflect on the self-embrace. Feel the warmth and peace of accepting yourself fully. Feel God's love for you and replace judgment with kindness. Rest in this self-acceptance. Open your eyes and carry this love with you throughout the rest of your day.

Day 3.   Spend five minutes reflecting on the choices that brought you to this point in your life. Breathe and embrace gratitude for the journey. Trust that God loves you and find peace in the present moment.

Day 4.   Spend five minutes reflecting on a choice you'll need to make in the next day. It can be a big choice or a simple one. Visualize your upcoming choice. Invite God's guidance and trust in divine wisdom. Release attachments and listen to your intuition. With God's help, see yourself making the choice aligned with your highest good.

Day 5.   Today, reflect on a routine choice, like what you will eat in the next day. Visualize yourself making choices that align with your best health and highest good. This is how you learn to make choices and trust God to give you the wisdom to make the right decisions.

CHAPTER 10
PRACTICING NONJUDGMENT

How I love Your instruction! It is my meditation all day long. Your commands make me wiser than my enemies, for they are always with me. I have more insight than all my teachers because Your decrees are my meditation.
Psalm 119:97-99 Holman Christian Standard Bible

"Can you believe our sales system crashed? This is awful!" Akar said, smearing beads of sweat across his brow.

"Is it?" Chantelle asked. Akar glared. "Consider practicing nonjudgment," Chantelle suggested, nonplussed.

"What?" Akar asked, scowling.

Chantelle told him this tale:

A farmer with a large tract only had an old mule to plough it. "How sad," his neighbors clucked.

The farmer said, "In all things, I am grateful."

Then one day the mule died. "How awful," his neighbors cried.

"Is it?" the farmer asked.

While walking his tract, the farmer discovered a badly beaten man under a hedge. "This is awful," cried his neighbors. "Leave him lest the bandits return!"

"Is it awful?" the farmer asked while nursing the man to health. It turned out the man was wealthy, and he sent the farmer a young stallion in thanks.

"Fantastic," yelled the fickle neighbors. "Good thing you helped him!"

"Was it?" asked the farmer."

When the farmer's son visited, he was riding the steed when it was spooked and bucked. The son fell on his head and died instantly.

"Oh no," cried the neighbors. "This is the worst!"

"Is it?" the farmer asked. "In all things, I am grateful." His daughter-in-law told him his son had a disease and was dying a slow, painful death. His son's worst fear had been the horrifying path that lay ahead.

The Takeaway

What if you don't rush to label things as good or bad, and accept that they just are?

Many of us are like the farmer's neighbors and rush to label situations. A core tenet of mindfulness is nonjudgment.

Acceptance without judgment recognizes that things just are. Each event wasn't inherently good or bad. It just was.

Being present without judgment includes resisting the urge to label events because all things work together in complex patterns that are difficult—if not impossible—to define in a single dimension. But the one thing we can know with certainty is that regardless of how they feel in the moment, all things work together for good for those that love God.

My Journal Reflections

So, when you find yourself in a circumstance that seems good, thank God. And when you find yourself in a circumstance that seems bad, thank God. Remember, nonjudgment is a powerful practice that helps cultivate compassion and foster deeper connections with God and others. Embrace the grace and wisdom He offers, and let His love guide you towards a mindset of acceptance and understanding.

Day 1.   Begin your five-minute meditation by centering yourself in God's unconditional love. Let go of any judgment or criticism towards yourself or others. Embrace the awareness that we are all created in His image, deserving of compassion and understanding.

Day 2.   In today's five-minute meditation, mentally focus on your breath, watching as you inhale and exhale. Acknowledge any judgmental thoughts or tendencies that arise. Instead of attaching to them, surrender them to God. Allow His love to fill your heart, replacing judgment with acceptance and forgiveness.

Day 3.   Visualize yourself in the presence of God, sitting together in a space of pure love and nonjudgment. Feel His divine embrace and imagine His gentle voice reminding you to let go of judgment and see others through His compassionate eyes.

Day 4.   During your meditation, practice observing your thoughts without judgment. As thoughts come and go, simply notice them without labeling them as good or bad. Allow God's presence to guide your awareness, fostering a sense of nonjudgmental acceptance.

Day 5.   Extend your practice of nonjudgment beyond your meditation session. Throughout your day, whenever you catch yourself judging others or yourself, pause and redirect your thoughts to God's perspective. Choose to see others through His lens of love, compassion, and acceptance.

CHAPTER 11

THE POWER OF
MANTRAS

*I will meditate on Your precepts and think about Your
ways.*

Psalm 119:15 Holman Christian Standard Bible

Every morning after brushing her teeth, Chantelle settles herself cross-legged on the meditation pillow in their glass sunroom. Today she rubs her bruised shin, where Dale kicked her during a nightmare. The first big challenge after they married was meshing her French and his American cultures. Dale suffers from post-traumatic stress disorder. Behind the façade of the happy military couple with three adorable boys and lovely suburban home lies pain. Chantelle adores Dale; he is the bravest man she knows. He has weathered the worst of heavy combat. She respects his dedication to country, but the cost to him and their family is dear.

With palms on her thighs, she closes her eyes and mentally watches her breath. She inhales peace and exhales stress. She begins with a prayer. "Good morning, Papa. I love You, I need You, and I exalt Your holy name. Please walk with me always, and throughout this day. Bless my babies and watch over them this day. Bless Dale and the work of his hands." She goes on to thank God for the good things He has done for specific friends and family, and she raises her concerns. She reflects on the day before without judgment and apologizes for her wrong thoughts or actions.

Transitioning to meditative reflection, she repeats a short phrase in her mind: "I choose love. I choose joy and peace this day."

With each repetition she focuses on the deeper meaning of each word. She visualizes herself treating Dale with love and compassion. She sees herself facing her volatile CEO, Gottfried, with calm. Sometimes it takes a long time to clearly visualize her intentions.

The Takeaway

Chantelle uses the power of prayer and intention to influence her daily actions. You can too.

First, we think, then we do, then we become.

Mindfulness meditation is less about doing and mostly about becoming—becoming calm and empowered from within no matter what's happening out there. It is about coming into the fullness of all the gifts you were born with.

The trouble for many of us is that we have been tricked into believing we are less than we are through repetitive negative messaging. Harness the same power of repetitive messaging to transform negative into positive belief systems. Build your psychological, emotional, and spiritual house on the rock of God's love for you. No matter what comes, that love will remain unshaken, and He will always be with you wherever you go.

My Journal Reflections

As you practice with mantras, allow these sacred words to become anchors for your mind, guiding your thoughts and bringing you closer to God's presence. Embrace the transformative power of repetitive affirmations, inviting His truth and love to resonate deeply within you. Begin with a prayer and a few deep breaths. Then set your alarm for five minutes and meditate on a topic below for five minutes.

Day 1.   Choose a God-centered mantra that resonates with you, such as "God is love" or "I am divinely guided." Repeat this mantra silently or aloud during your meditation, allowing its truth to permeate your being and align your thoughts with God's presence and grace. Repeat it, going deeper into its meaning with every repetition.

Day 2.   Reflect on a Scripture verse that carries a powerful message of God's truth and love. Repeat this verse as a mantra, allowing its words to sink deep into your heart and mind. Let it be a source of strength and inspiration, reminding you of God's faithfulness.

Day 3. Select a mantra that affirms your trust in God's plan, such as "I surrender to God's will" or "I trust in His timing." Repeat this mantra with conviction and surrender, releasing any need for control and embracing the peace that comes from trusting in His divine guidance.

Day 4. Use a gratitude-focused mantra that acknowledges God's blessings in your life, such as "Thank you, God, for your abundant grace" or "I am grateful for all the ways God blesses me." Repeat this mantra with a spirit of gratitude, recognizing His goodness and opening your heart to receive more blessings.

Day 5. Create a personal mantra that encapsulates your desired connection with God, such as "I am one with God's love and light" or "I and my Father are one." Repeat this mantra with intention, allowing it to affirm your identity as a beloved child of God and to strengthen your spiritual connection.

CHAPTER 12

TAME YOUR RACING MIND

I am awake through each watch of the night to meditate on Your promise.

Psalm 119:148 Holman Christian Standard Bible

Akar dragged himself into the meditation room. He was drained. His pants sagged over his flat bottom, his tie was crooked, and even his thick salt-and pepper silver hair fell limp. But when he entered the room, he instantly felt a sense of calm positive energy. He had meditated in the morning but was glad he returned that night.

He read a bit and opened with a quick prayer, "Dear God, be here with me." Then he set his alarm for five minutes. He began with deep-breathing exercises, inhaling, holding the breath, exhaling.

After three or four repetitions, he was ready for his reflection. To counteract Gottfried's negativity, he chose a chant. With each repetition, he dug deeper and visualized how he would move through the day from a place of self-trust.

It started out well enough but quickly derailed. *I trust my judgment. I trust my judgment. Chantelle is out of town. I'll eat lunch at my desk. No, I should take a mindful break.* Then he caught himself. *Oh, wait, I trust my judgment. I trust my judgment. I'll stop by the grocery store, so I can take sandwiches to work. Oh wait, I trust my judgment.*

After forever, he thought, *my alarm is broken because I've been struggling for an hour!* He waited for the alarm to sound. Finally, Akar peeked and realized it had only been two minutes!

The Takeaway

Akar's is a common experience. Five minutes feels like forever, and it's a fight to discipline your thoughts. Don't be discouraged. Even seasoned meditators have days like this. With time and consistency, it gets easier. If you spend the entire time fighting distraction, simply think, *Self, I didn't do so well today, but I'll be back to try again.* A significant challenge in learning the habit of meditation is simply overcoming the discouragement and disappointment in yourself as you try and feel as if you're failing to tame your racing mind. A critical component of mindfulness is non-judgment and that includes (perhaps most of all) the nonjudgment of self. Master the art of showing up consistently, and the rest will take care of itself.

My Journal Reflections

Remember, the obstacles you encounter during meditation are not barriers but invitations for growth and deeper connection with God. Embrace these challenges with an open heart and a spirit of surrender, knowing that God's presence is with you every step of the way. Begin with a prayer and a few deep breaths. Then set your alarm for five minutes and meditate on a topic below for five minutes.

Day 1.   During today's meditation, focus on a topic, and acknowledge any distractions or obstacles that arise during your meditation, whether it's wandering thoughts, restlessness, or external noise. Surrender these challenges to God, inviting His presence to help you find stillness and peace amidst the chaos.

Day 2.   Invite God to sit with you during your meditation. Set an intention before your meditation to release any expectations or judgments about the quality of your practice. Embrace the understanding that every moment spent in God's presence is valuable, regardless of any perceived obstacles. Trust that He is present and working in every aspect of your meditation.

Day 3.   Select a mantra that speaks to you for today's meditation. When faced with a busy mind or racing thoughts, gently bring your focus back to your breath or a sacred word. Use this anchor to reconnect with God's presence and bring a sense of calm and clarity to your meditation. Trust that even a few moments of centeredness can create a sacred space for God to work within you.

Day 4.   Today, visualize some aspect to the day ahead and visualize you behaving at your best. If physical discomfort arises during meditation, approach it with patience and compassion. Adjust your posture, find a comfortable position, and allow yourself to be present with any sensations that arise. Offer these moments of discomfort as an offering to God, surrendering them and seeking His comfort and guidance.

Day 5.   During today's meditation, when external noises or disturbances interrupt your meditation, view them as opportunities to practice acceptance and adaptability. Embrace these moments as invitations to invite God's peace into the midst of the external chaos. Trust that He is present, guiding you through the obstacles and bringing you closer to Him.

CHAPTER 13

THE BENEFITS OF MEDITATION

I am awake through each watch of the night to meditate on Your promise.

Isaiah 40:31 Holman Christian Standard Bible

"Chantelle, this meditation thing is hard," Akar said, happy his friend was back as he loped beside her. He was suited up for a client meeting and tried meditation beforehand. But he kept worrying about the meeting.

"The hardest part is establishing the habit and sticking to it," Chantelle said.

Flashes of Chantelle's composure in myriad difficult situations flew through Akar's mind. With a new openness he said, "Remind me why I'm doing this again."

Chantelle didn't miss a beat. "When you pray, you talk to God. Meditating on God and His word creates space for God to talk to you. Meditation can increase your wisdom and discernment, in addition to increasing your calm and peace."

Chantelle cocked a dark brow at Akar. "Do you agree that God is always with you?"

Akar nodded vigorously.

"But you don't always feel His presence."

Akar nodded again.

Chantelle continued, "To be sure, God is always walking beside us. To the extent that we don't feel it, it's most often because we haven't taken the time or effort to connect with Him. When you increase your ability to experience your real closeness to God, you are better able to experience and *know* who you are as a child of the divine creator. Once you see that, you transcend race, color, and all the material judgments we place on each other as human beings. Once you know who you really are, you will be far less susceptible to the petty ups and downs of this earthly existence."

The Takeaway

Benefits vary and depend on consistent practice. Studies have shown that you can reap great benefits of meditation with as few as twelve minutes a day and ideally, twenty to thirty minutes once or twice a day over an extended period. Meditation is not a quick fix; it is a daily journey of becoming. God-centered meditation can result in a flourishing as a tree flourishes when nurtured by water and a constant source of life.

Don't be discouraged if it doesn't feel like anything is happening. Grass grows even though you can't see the process. Just start with five minutes each morning. Some days will feel like you're fighting to be still every second. Other days you will feel the warm bliss of meditation and won't want to stop. Let the blissful days fuel the hard days. And above all else, just keep at it.

My Journal Reflections

Remember, the journey of faith includes moments of perceived absence or uncertainty. Stay committed to your meditation practice, trusting in God's unchanging love and knowing that He is always present, whether felt or not. Embrace the beauty of the journey and the transformative power of consistent practice. Begin with a prayer and a few deep breaths. Then set your alarm for five minutes and meditate on a topic below for five minutes.

Day 1. In today's meditation, even if you don't feel God's presence, trust that He is always with you, regardless of your perception. You can recite a mantra such as "Dear God, I know you're here," or "I know you are with me always." Embrace the faith that His love and guidance are constant, even when they may not be immediately felt. Stay committed to your meditation practice, knowing that God's presence transcends your emotions or sensations.

Day 2. Today, use your meditation practice as a way to seek God rather than solely relying on feeling His presence. Shift your focus from seeking a specific experience to cultivating a deeper connection with Him. Trust that the consistency of your practice will create space for His presence to unfold in unexpected ways.

Day 3.   As you meditate today, remember that the purpose of meditation is not solely to feel God's presence, but also to develop a sense of inner stillness and awareness. Even in moments when His presence may not be palpable, use this time to quiet your mind, listen to His gentle whisper, and cultivate a heart that is receptive to His guidance.

Day 4.   Today, be still and embrace the opportunity to surrender your need for immediate gratification and practice patience in your meditation. Trust that God's presence works in His perfect timing. Remain committed to your practice, knowing that even in the stillness where you may not perceive His presence, He is actively shaping and transforming your soul.

Day 5.   In today's meditation, cultivate gratitude for the mere opportunity to engage in meditation and connect with God, regardless of how you feel in the moment. Shift your focus from seeking a particular experience to being grateful for the sacred space you create in your practice. Trust that God honors your dedication and will reveal His presence in His divine way and timing.

P

CHAPTER 14

NOTHING IS HAPPENING

When the servant of the man of God got up early and went out, he discovered an army with horses and chariots surrounding the city. So he asked Elisha, "Oh, my master, what are we to do?" Elisha said, "Don't be afraid, for those who are with us outnumber those who are with them." Then Elisha prayed, "Lord, please open his eyes and let him see." So the Lord opened the servant's eyes. He looked and saw that the mountain was covered with horses and chariots of fire all around Elisha.

2 Kings 6:15-17 Holman Christian Standard Bible

"Why do you look like someone stole your dance moves and hit the stage first?" Chantelle asked Akar.

"Nothing's happening," Akar lamented. "I've been at this meditation thing for three months, and nothing's changed. I love them to bits, but Zahra and the kids still get on my nerves, and Gottfried's still tirading. I wanted to feel unflappable like you, but it's not happening." He sat down heavily on the bright blue bench near the Sunderland campus auditorium and rolled up his shirt sleeves. Slouching in discouragement, he said, "Maybe this meditation thing just isn't for me."

Chantelle patted his forearm. "You're doing great, Akar. You just can't see it," she said. When he looked at her skeptically, Chantelle asked, "When was the last time you felt really upset about Gottfried?"

Akar paused. It had been weeks.

The Takeaway

Just because you don't see progress doesn't mean nothing is happening.

The internal evolution of becoming isn't obvious to the becomer. Akar didn't realize it, but over time, he was less upset every time Gottfried threw a tantrum. Gottfried hadn't changed, but Akar's reaction did. Akar also didn't notice that even when he did get upset, the peaks of his anxiety were less pronounced. Only when Chantelle pointed it out did Akar see the change.

Practicing mindfulness is like physical exercise. You don't see your muscles develop, but one day you flex, and there they are. Also, the more you practice, the stronger your concentration and focus become, and the less you are buffeted by the daily ups and downs of life. One day you will turn around and realize that even when you don't feel the warm tingling presence of God, you have an unshakable faith of His presence. And the more you walk with Him, the greater your clarity about where you are in life, your spiritual purpose, and what you need to learn. The more you meditate, the more you can be filled with the fruits of the Spirit – love, joy, patience, goodness, faithfulness, gentleness, and self-control. All this can translate into deeper peace and contentment.

Don't stare at your mental biceps each day, looking for signs of growth. Just focus on the discipline of showing up every day and taking time for yourself. The results will come in time. Five minutes gets you started. The greater your consistency and concentration, the better your results.

My Journal Reflections

Remember, the journey of meditation is a lifelong process. Cultivate patience, trusting in God's timing and divine plan. Commit to your practice with unwavering dedication, knowing that each moment spent in His presence brings you closer to experiencing His love and transformative power. Begin with a prayer and a few deep breaths. Then set your alarm for five minutes and meditate on a topic below for five minutes.

Day 1.　Today, meditate on God's unwavering love for you. Embrace the power of consistency in your meditation practice, knowing that God honors your commitment and dedication. Trust that even on days when it feels challenging or uneventful, each moment spent in meditation draws you closer to God's loving presence.

Day 2.   In today's meditation, reflect on the topic of surrendering to God's plan and trusting in His divine timing. Set a clear intention to cultivate patience and perseverance in your meditation practice. Recognize that growth takes time and that the fruits of your practice may not be immediately apparent.

Day 3.   Focus your meditation on cultivating a heart of gratitude and recognizing God's blessings in your life. During moments of restlessness or distraction in meditation, gently bring your focus back to God's presence. Let go of any expectations or judgments about your progress and simply be present with Him. Practice redirecting your attention with grace and compassion, knowing that each moment of refocusing strengthens your ability to be present.

Day 4.   Meditate on the topic of finding peace and stillness in God's presence, even amidst life's challenges. Use affirmations or sacred words as tools to anchor your focus during meditation. Repeat phrases such as "I am patient in God's presence" or "I commit to my practice with steadfast dedication." Allow these affirmations to guide your mind back to the present moment, reinforcing your commitment to consistent practice.

Day 5.   Reflect on the topic of seeking God's guidance and wisdom in decision-making through your meditation practice. Reflect on the transformative power of steady, devoted meditation over time. Recall moments when you felt God's presence deeply during your practice and allow those memories to fuel your commitment. Trust that through consistency, you create a foundation for God's love and guidance to flow more effortlessly into your life.

THE
SEASONS
OF
YOUR
LIFE

DARK

Finding the Light When Darkness Has Fallen

The meditations in this season are best used when you are experiencing difficulties in life. You were afraid a storm was gathering on the horizon, but you were wrong; it was a full-blown hurricane! In the dark of your life's night, those things that were sliding sideways plunged into what felt like your own valley of the shadow of death:

Join our mindfulness support group in which four strangers become friends. Each has a personal struggle that drove them to join the group.

- Barry is struggling to accept the demise of his marriage.
- Singita is trying to cope with difficult family relationships.
- Rashad and Brianna celebrated their twins heading off to college. Now what?

Hopefully you will see your struggles in the journeys of the four and how you can harness the power of mindfulness meditation to face the ups and downs of each day.

The dark season is when many people are most vulnerable and most likely to retreat into a shell, forsaking God, daily routines and good habits. And this is the time when it is most beneficial to spend energy on mindfulness meditation.

Take comfort in knowing that you're not the first person to encounter difficulty or to struggle. Notice how the members of the Mindful in 5 support group seek God's help, talk to Him through their fears, and sometimes just lament about their situations. Give yourself permission to be honest with God about how you feel when life isn't going well. Crying out to God and being vulnerable with Him not only strengthens your bond, but it also connects your hopelessness with the hope that God gives. We all experience seasons of grief and sadness, The first step is to bring it to God. Lean on Him. He won't sit in judgment and cast you down. Create space for Him to comfort and help you.

Like these four friends, hopefully you will come to see that it's not what's happening out there that defines you. It's who you're praying to, what's in your spirit, and what's between your own two ears.

Use the reflections in this dark season to help you step into your new paradigm of self-empowerment and hope, no matter what is happening in your life.

CHAPTER 1

TAKE TIME

Be strong and courageous; don't be terrified or afraid of them. For it is the Lord your God who goes with you; He will not leave you or forsake you.

Deuteronomy 31:6 Holman Christian Standard Bible

Barry Miles instinctively grabbed for his five-year-old son as the plane instantly dropped ten feet. "Weeee!" squealed little Navesh in delight. After another ten feet, passengers began screaming and crying. A storm pummeled the plane, tossing the jetliner about like a sparrow.

The captain's reassuring voice beamed through the intercom. "We are experiencing significant turbulence and loss of cabin pressure.

Oxygen masks above your seat will deploy. Please place the mask on first, and then assist other passengers."

Barry looked at his son and sent up a quick prayer, "Dear God, I know you're here. Please save us.". The gleeful child turned wailing boy mirrored the palpable terror of the fellow passengers. Navesh began hyperventilating and wheezing, his asthma kicking in.

Ignoring his own mask and the dizziness on the edges of his consciousness, Barry reached for his son. He didn't appreciate how fast the air was changing in the cabin and that he only had seconds to put his mask on to feed oxygen to his brain. Just as he pulled down his son's mask, hypoxia overcame him, and everything faded to black.

The Takeaway

If you are not good to yourself, you may be no good to others.

Barry's experience is not uncommon, especially for parents. Many people view time as a luxury. But spiritual examples demonstrate repeatedly that it is important to take time away from our responsibilities to spend time alone with God. Even He *rested* on the seventh day after creation. Jesus spent 40 days and nights alone with his father in the desert. Cultures across the world bear examples of those who have and continue to spend countless hours in meditation.

Taking time for yourself is not selfish, and you should not feel guilty about it. It is especially important in your darkest season, when you need to be most centered to weather storms that could destabilize you. Ensuring your own wellness is also the best assurance that you will be able to serve others.

Plug into the celestial battery and use that to draw the emotional strength you need to get through each day – especially during difficult times.

In this moment, be present with yourself. Each of us receives the same twenty-four hours each day. If you spend eight to twelve hours working, isn't it only fair that you take at least five minutes for yourself? Be still. For yourself. Right now.

My Journal Reflections

Open with a prayer and spend at least five minutes with God in silent meditation first thing each morning for at least 5 days this week. There is no one right way to pray. Go to your quiet spot, take a posture that feels best. You can recite a scripted prayer, or just talk to God in the language of your heart. Consider expressing gratitude, consulting God, asking for what you need, and praying for others. Three critical components are that you are reverend, authentic, and humble. Don't try to hide or fake it. He can see right through you every time. He understands you better than you know yourself. He will always love you whether you're naughty or good, so just be yourself. Use these topics and your journal to guide your thoughts.

Day 1.   Start with a few deep breaths. After your prayer, take five minutes to meditate on the following scripture: *Be still and know that I am God.* With each inhale and exhale, reflect more deeply on this scripture. Give yourself this gift of time to just be still with God and breathe.

Day 2.   Take five minutes to reflect on the activities of your typical day that take up all your time. If you feel pressured to give all your time away, ask God to help you identify the source of this pressure so you can address it.

Day 3.   Today, visualize your day and reflect on how you can find moments throughout your day to connect with God and listen for His voice. Remember that He is with you always. Reconnecting can be as simple as taking a moment to remember that He is there and say hello.

Day 4.   Today when you close your eyes, relax. Reflect on the luxury of giving yourself time. Ask God to remind you of the activities that bring you joy. Feel the sensations of relaxation and contentment. Recognize the importance of prioritizing self-care. When you open your eyes and carry this awareness with you.

Day 5.   Close your eyes and breathe deeply. Reflect on making time for daily meditation with God. Visualize a peaceful space and the benefits it brings. Envision overcoming obstacles with determination. Feel the anticipation and love in this practice. Open your eyes and carry this intention with you, nurturing your spiritual journey.

CHAPTER 2

SHOW UP

The Angel of the Lord found her by a spring of water in the wilderness, the spring on the way to Shur. He said, "Hagar, slave of Sarai, where have you come from and where are you going?"

Genesis 16:7-8 Holman Christian Standard Bible

Cassie watched Singita, the beautiful, petite Indian woman, manipulate a completely jumbled Rubik's Cube with speed that blurred her long red fingernails and the multicolored squares. Singita had arrived early. Cassie was leader of the *Mindful in 5* peer support group, which provided a haven to work through difficult transitions. Today was their first meeting.

Cassie was a tall, pale ruler of a woman whose vaguely ginger curls contrasted to the fiery red buzz cut Barry Miles wore when he burst into the room. A taut barrel on broomsticks, Barry was broad and chiseled. His every movement declared prior military training, now a little soft. "Hi, y'all," he said as he flashed open his coat to blind everyone with an enormous belt buckle declaring "Texas." Red plaid shirt, faded jeans, and large furry boots completed the ensemble.

Cassie pretended not to notice as he appraised her flowy flannel shirt and skirt. It was dusty brown today, but she had the same outfit in camouflage green and slate gray. Only her intelligent green eyes with flecks of shooting amber and her conflagration of curls that she tried to tame in a knot at the nape of her neck gave away the fire within her.

After Barry came Nandi Chaya, Fiona Darby, and Jillian and Gene Adams. Their gait and clothing created impressions before they ever spoke.

The Takeaway

You may have heard the adage, "You never get a second chance to make a first impression." As the group session opens, we see how different individuals show up in the same room.

And so, it is the same with each of us.

The impressions we make are defined by how we show up in the world.

Even as Cassie watched her new group members show up, she was making her own impressions on them and they on her. What is the

impression you want to make in every space where you show up? When you show up, what does it say about where you have come from and where you are going?

My Journal Reflections

Open with a prayer and spend at least five minutes with God in silent meditation first thing each morning for at least 5 days this week. Remember, meditation provides a sacred space for introspection and alignment with God's will. Use these prompts to explore how you can show up as a reflection of His love, grace, and truth in your interactions with others. May your time of meditation inspire you to bring more light and goodness to the world around you.

Day 1.   During your meditation, reflect on how you show up in the world and the qualities you want to embody. Consider how you can bring more love, compassion, and kindness to your interactions with colleagues, friends, and family members.

Day 2.   Today, focus your meditation on the impact you want to have on others. Visualize yourself radiating God's light and love, inspiring and uplifting those around you. Set the intention to be a vessel of His grace and reflect His goodness in your words and actions.

Day 3.   Meditate on the topic of authenticity and being true to yourself in your relationships. Reflect on how you can align your thoughts, words, and actions with your core values and beliefs. Ask God to guide you in being genuine and transparent with others.

Day 4.   During your five-minute meditation, contemplate the power of forgiveness and reconciliation. Reflect on any relationships that may be strained or in need of healing. Pray for the wisdom and strength to extend forgiveness, seek reconciliation, and demonstrate God's love in challenging circumstances.

Day 5.   Focus your meditation on gratitude for the people in your life. Reflect on the blessings they bring and the support they provide. Consider how you can express your appreciation and love to them more fully, allowing God's love to flow through your interactions and relationships.

CHAPTER 3

GOD-CENTERED MEDITATION IS FOR EVERYONE

My mouth speaks wisdom; my heart's meditation brings understanding.

Psalm 49:3 Holman Christian Standard Bible

At six o'clock, Cassie cleared her throat and welcomed the eight seated attendees. As she spoke, the last four stragglers scuttled in and quickly took their seats. She pushed her large tortoiseshell glasses up her nose and announced in her smooth voice that the group would begin with five minutes of silent meditation. Thereafter, each attendee was invited to share their spiritual walk.

"I'm a recovering alcoholic. Step three of AA involved deciding to turn my will and my life to my Higher Power. I want to get to know Him better!" Barry Miles jumped in without hesitation.

"I love God, and my roots are in Hinduism. I go to a meditation group in Minneapolis where our services include readings from the Bhagavad Gita, the New Testament from the Bible, and time for silent meditation," Singita chirped, casting a perfectly shaded but unimpressed side eye at Barry. The now perfectly solved Rubik's Cube rested in her lap, blending into her salwar kameez, a splash of fresh color in the pale room.

Cassie cocked her head. Ever since the first day when Singita turned up her nose at Barry's funky boots and mismatched would-be cowboy getup, Cassie had noticed the simmering disdain Singita held for Barry. Cassie smiled to herself.

"We go to church…sometimes," said Brianna Patterson casting an accusatory glance at her husband, Rashad.

"I don't know much about spirituality, but I'd like to learn," Fiona Darby said in her strong English accent.

Nandi Chaya said thoughtfully, "I'm from Zimbabwe, where Western spirituality and traditional ancestral worship live alongside each other. Both sides believe in the existence of one ultimate creator.

"Frankly I'm not sure about this God stuff," Jillian Adams said with a toss of her jet-black bob. "I've had a lot of tragedy in my life, and He never showed up to help me. So, I don't even know if this God you speak of even exists."

"Really?" Barry asked in genuine surprise. "I thought all you Asians were spiritual."

Several eyebrows shot up. Cassie's eyes were calm summer leaves infiltrated with flecks of golden sunlight as they bounced between Barry and Jillian.

Jillian's modelesque placid face clouded as a frown marred her forehead. "He made me come," she barked, with an angry flick of her head towards her husband, Gene. Light bounced off his scalp, through the strips of his comb over. His weathered, pockmarked face was vacant. He didn't seem to be listening.

The Takeaway

No matter where you are in your own spiritual journey, don't rely on others to craft your relationship. Religious teachings can provide guidance, but nothing replaces the truth of experiencing God for yourself. Meditation can serve as a tool to connect you with the Divine so you can develop your own understanding of God. Through meditation, you can gain greater clarity about the challenges of life and your thwarted expectations, creating a deeper sense of inner peace, clarity, and spiritual insight.

My Journal Reflections

Open with a prayer and spend at least five minutes in silent meditation with God for at least five days this week. Remember that mindfulness and meditation are pathways to experiencing God's presence within and around you. Embrace these practices with an open heart, and allow yourself to connect deeply with the divine in your own unique way.

Day 1.   Sit in your quiet place, close your eyes, and take a few deep breaths. In your meditation, embrace the depth of your personal relationship with God. Reflect on His unique presence in your life and meditate on the topic of deepening that connection even further. Seek His guidance and wisdom as you explore ways to cultivate a more intimate and vibrant relationship with Him.

Day 2.   During your meditation, focus on the topic of surrendering to God's will. Embrace the beauty of aligning your desires with His divine plan. Reflect on how you can release control and trust in His loving guidance, allowing His purpose to unfold in your life.

Day 3.   Meditate on the topic of gratitude for God's blessings and faithfulness. Reflect on the specific ways He has shown His love and provision in your life. Allow gratitude to fill your heart and express your thankfulness to Him in prayer and meditation.

Day 4.   Reflect on the topic of seeking God's presence in the midst of life's challenges. Meditate on how you can turn to Him for strength, comfort, and guidance during difficult times. Explore ways to deepen your reliance on His love and grace, trusting that He will carry you through any adversity.

Day 5.   During your meditation, contemplate the topic of living out your faith in daily life. Reflect on how you can embody God's love, compassion, and truth in your thoughts, words, and actions. Seek His guidance to be a living testament of His grace and an instrument of His peace to those around you.

CHAPTER 4

ESCAPING PAIN

The wise endowed with equanimity of intellect, abandon attachment to the fruits of actions, which bind one to the cycle of life and death. By working in such consciousness, they attain the state beyond all suffering.
Bhagavad Gita (Bhagavad Gita): Chapter 2, Verse 51

Singita volunteered to go first. "Hi, my name is Singita Patel." Cassie's curls bobbed, accompanied by an encouraging smile.

"Hi, Singita," everyone said in unison.

Singita seemed still, but her ponytail trembled. ""I-I ..." She tried again. "I lost my appä, my father." Her large ebony eyes were moist pools, but she rushed on. "I think Appä always believed his friends and neighbors were beneath him. After I obeyed his command to apply for

his US citizenship, he denounced everyone in our small community in Chennai. When the immigration application was denied, he disowned me, forcing Ammä, my brother, and sisters to choose sides."

Unable to continue, Singita lapsed into silence. Her perfectly sculpted brows flattened into a scowl that contorted her smooth, honey-hued face. Then with a vigorous shake of her head, Singita declared, "I shouldn't be going through this. I don't want to talk about this." The group sat in silence while Cassie made sure Singita had no more to say.

Then she began. "In the Disney movie *Finding Nemo,* there is a scene where the father, Marlon, is searching for his son, Nemo. A school of fish tell his sidekick, Dory, that when they arrive at this trench, they should swim through it, not over it."

Cassie noted Singita's confusion and continued. "The trench is deep and scary-looking, complete with skeletons of long-dead fish. Marlon takes one look and decides they should swim over it. Over Dory's objections, he tricks her into going over it to the bright, sun-drenched sea overhead. The flaw in Marlon's escapism is almost immediately apparent, when the two little fish are beset by a swarm of venomous jellyfish."

The Takeaway

Surviving a breakup or dealing with an involuntary life change is a lot like this. There you sit, facing a menacing trench of agony, disgruntlement, embarrassment, disillusionment, and a ball in your stomach of negative feelings you can't even put into words.

The God lover's journey is not graced with perpetual rainbows and flowers. Even in the Bible, we see evidence of deep grief and suffering.

Like Singita, you have a choice. Do you evade the trench? Surely the blue skies of alcohol, new relationships, retail therapy, or even drug addiction are easier than going through that trench. Right?

My Journal Reflections

Start with a prayer then spend at least five minutes with God in silent meditation first thing each morning for at least five days this week. You can journal after your meditation for deeper clarity.

Day 1.   For the next five minutes, go within and mentally lay at God's feet your terror, rage, disappointment, blame, self-doubt, and all the emotions you have been experiencing. And breathe.

Day 2.   Today, ask God to show you the truth about your trench. Do you have a trench you have been avoiding? Can you examine it without fear or self-judgment?

Day 3.   Today, practice vulnerability and share with God how you feel about your trench. You don't need words and you don't need to have absolute clarity. Just open your heart and allow the feelings to flow. He will understand the complexity of your emotions – perhaps even better than you can.

Day 4.   Ask God to help you unpack the reasons you are most frightened of going through your trench. Don't undertake this meditation if it will be triggering or harmful for you. Don't judge yourself by thinking you should be better or stronger. Accept yourself just as you are.

Day 5.   In your meditation time today, ask God to illuminate in your life the negative consequences of your avoiding your trench. What is it costing you? What is it holding you back from?

CHAPTER 5
FACE PAIN

Do not be afraid, for you will not be put to shame; don't be humiliated, for you will not be disgraced. For you will forget the shame of your youth, and you will no longer remember the disgrace of your widowhood.
Isaiah 54:4 Holman Christian Standard Bible

"What's wrong with pain avoidance?" Barry demanded. "Between car racin', rodeo, and, and…" Barry caught himself as he saw the women glaring, "well, you can drown a lot of pain!" Beside him, Rashad Patterson guffawed while his wife, Brianna, glowered.

"Barry, right?" Cassie asked.

"Yup. Barry Andrew Miles. *BAM!* From Danville, Kentucky."

Singita frowned. "Your belt screams Texas."

"I wish I was from Texas!" Barry slapped a big hairy hand on his big solid thigh, and gales of laughter shook his robust frame.

Cassie continued, "It might seem easier. But soon the venomous jellyfish of negative consequences from addictions, avoidance, and your own unresolved negative emotions sting. Emotional recovery varies for everyone. And there's no shortcut."

Cassie surveyed the group. Tugging her drab shirt, she said, "Years ago, I got divorced." There were surprised gasps from the attendees.

Cassie nodded. "Shocking! I'm such a nice person, how could that possibly happen? I get that all the time. It's why I became a counselor. My DivorceCare coach said it could take half the length of the relationship to get over it. I was married for fifteen years. What?" Cassie smiled at the slack jaws.

"I was single for ten years before I remarried. Determined never to encounter the divorce trench again, I took the time to heal and become this woman, to shed my negative cycles, and attract the kind of relationship I wanted. My goal is to turn all of you into mindful ninjas so you can each conquer your trench. Going through that scary trench for all those years paid off in more ways than I could have ever dreamed."

The Takeaway

You attract what you reflect.

Sometimes bad things happen to us for no discernable reason. But often, we orchestrate our own misfortune based on the decisions we make,

or the decisions other people make that impact our lives. God is not a helicopter parent who swoops in to save you from yourself or others just in time. He might allow you to fall down and struggle, but He will nonetheless help you through it if you're brave enough to take the journey and ask for His help.

Cassie is happily married to her soul mate, Alan. What she gained from going through the trench was priceless. Don't go over the trench. Go through it.

My Journal Reflections

Start with a prayer then spend at least five minutes with God in silent meditation first thing each morning for at least five days this week. In these meditations, allow God's love and presence to guide you as you face pain with compassion, forgiveness, and grace. May your time of reflection bring healing, restoration, and a deeper understanding of the transformative power of God's love in your life.

Day 1. During your meditation, embrace the power of God's love to heal and transform pain. Reflect on the pain you carry. Pray for the strength to face and process these wounds with compassion and forgiveness, allowing God's love to bring healing and restoration.

Day 2. In today's meditation, courageously face the decisions or actions that have contributed to your own pain. Reflect on the role you have played in creating or perpetuating difficult situations. Seek God's loving presence and guidance as you explore ways to take responsibility, learn from these experiences, and make choices aligned with His wisdom and grace.

Day 3.   During your meditation, reflect on the lessons and growth opportunities that lie within the experiences that have caused you pain. Pray for the strength to face any guilt or regret with self-compassion and forgiveness, allowing God's grace to bring healing and transformation to those aspects of your life.

Day 4.   Focus your meditation on the topic of self-compassion. Embrace God's unconditional love and extend that love to yourself, especially in moments of pain and struggle. Practice self-forgiveness and offer yourself the same grace and compassion that God extends to you.

Day 5.   During your meditation, contemplate the topic of surrendering your pain to God's loving care. Visualize placing your burdens at the feet of God, trusting in His divine wisdom and timing. Seek His guidance and comfort, knowing that He can use our pain for greater purposes and transform it into something beautiful.

CHAPTER 6

COPING

To everything there is a season, a time for every purpose under heaven: a time to break down, and a time to build up; a time to weep, and a time to laugh; a time to mourn, and a time to dance; a time to embrace, and a time to refrain from embracing; a time to gain, and a time to lose; a time to love, and a time to hate; a time of war, and a time of peace.

Ecclesiastes 3:1, 3-6, 8 King James Version

Prompted by Cassie to reflect on something they loved, Barry had jumped in to talk about how much he loved his legal practice as a junior partner at a prominent law firm. Brianna cut him off when she yelped

in surprise as fur slithered around her dainty ankles. Shadow The Cat hissed as Cassie scooped him up. With a bite-sized chunk missing from one ear, pink crepe skin exposed by patches of missing gray fur, the cat looked as if he'd lost a battle with one of his bigger cousins. With his one insolent eye, the cat blinked at Brianna. Brianna shuddered. "You call that thing Shadow?" she asked.

"Shadow The Cat," said Cassie.

"Shadow?"

"Shadow The Cat," said Cassie.

Brianna let it go. "That's why we're here. We need a way through the trench." Her smile was brittle from years of bristling at her husband, Rashad. "Our twins left for college. The transition is … difficult."

Rashad chimed in, "Yeah, eighteen years ago Brianna went from being a wife to a mom, and that's all she's been since." His grin belied the bite in his tone. "Now that she's lost the kids, she wants her husband back." His amber eyes blazed as he patted her limp hand resting in his with angry vigor. Cassie quirked a brow.

"Funny," said Barry, cocking his head, "you look like the perfect Black suburban couple. I'd have never guessed y'all got marital problems."

The Takeaway

How do you maintain calm in the face of negative changes you can't control?

Control what you can and let go of the rest.

Accept what you can't control. Brianna and Rashad couldn't prevent their twins from growing up. Identify small and big things you can do in response to any given situation and do them. Brianna and Rashad can rediscover each other and their marriage—if they both want to.

Ask God to help you identify what you can do and put a plan in place for accomplishing your aspirations. Once you have that plan, release to God the events you can't control. Trust Him.

My Journal Reflections

Start with a prayer then spend at least five minutes with God in silent meditation for at least five days this week. It's easy to read this week's reflections but some of them may be difficult to get your head around. Return to them as often as necessary and lean into your journaling to help you. May these meditation prompts inspire you to embrace the power of surrender and discernment, enabling you to navigate life with grace, faith, and trust in God's loving guidance.

Day 1.   During your meditation, reflect on the aspects of your life that you have the power to change and improve. Seek God's guidance in discerning the areas where action is needed. Pray for the strength and wisdom to make the necessary changes, trusting in His support and provision along the way.

Day 2.   Focus your meditation on surrendering the outcomes and circumstances that are beyond your control. Bring to mind the situations or challenges that weigh heavily on your heart. Surrender them to God, releasing the need to control and trusting in His divine plan. Embrace the peace that comes from knowing He is in control and will work all things for your highest good.

Day 3.   Meditate on the topic of discernment, seeking God's guidance to distinguish between what you can change and what you need to surrender. Reflect on the areas of your life where you may be holding onto control out of fear or resistance. Open your heart to God's loving presence, inviting His wisdom to guide your decisions and actions.

Day 4.   In today's meditation, reflect on the Serenity Prayer during your meditation, repeating the words: "God, grant me the serenity to accept the things I cannot change, courage to change the things I can, and wisdom to know the difference." Embrace the message of surrender and empowerment, trusting that God will equip you to navigate life's challenges with grace and resilience.

Day 5.   During your meditation, visualize yourself letting go of the burdens of control. Picture your hands releasing the things you cannot change, lifting them up to God's loving care. Embrace a sense of liberation and peace as you surrender, trusting in His divine plan and the abundant blessings He has in store for you.

CHAPTER 7

FINANCIAL WORRIES

How long, Lord, must I call for help, but [Y]ou do not listen? Or cry out to [Y]ou, "Violence!" but [Y]ou do not save? Why do [Y]ou make me look at injustice? Why do [Y]ou tolerate wrongdoing? Destruction and violence are before me; there is strife, and conflict abounds.

Habakkuk 1:1-3 New International Version

Barry's broad chest constricted as he stared at the child support calculation for his sons. "Dear God, what am I going to do?" He muttered more to himself than to God.

The boys were only seven and five years old; he'd go bankrupt! He felt so positive when he left the last group session that he thought nothing could touch him. But now he yearned for a drink, even after a decade of sobriety. *God, I could really use a drink right now,* he thought. Fortunately there was no alcohol in his home and he was too weak with fear to go find some.

He could scarcely afford the divorce lawyer who sent him this proposal, and these numbers represented the best-case scenario. Ironically, as a lawyer himself, he understood how costly a support battle would be. His father-in-law, Mr. Gupta, was wealthy, Indian, and had never liked Barry. His eldest daughter marrying a Caucasian was a deep insult. Burying Barry in a mountain of expenses would delight him. Barry would have difficulty paying his bills, and that was before his three useless brothers called to mooch, which they always did. Barry placed the document facedown and walked away. *I can't think about this right now,* he decided. Soon, panic overwhelmed him and all he could do was lay on the couch, immobilized by fear. *God help me,* was all he could think over and over again in his mind.

The Takeaway

Finances can be stressful. Fights about money are still touted as a key contributor to divorce. Sometimes life takes an unexpected turn. A divorce, job loss, pandemic, medical diagnosis, an accident, or a death in the family can move you from financial stability to insecurity overnight.

Being mindful about money management includes understanding your motivations and being intentional about your spending. This is especially true when faced with a significant financial hurdle.

You can't address what you don't acknowledge.

First, face the problem head-on and quantify it. There are many books, guides, and tools that cover every aspect of financial planning. Whether you are digging yourself out of a hole or coasting to financial independence, there are resources to assist you. Take the first mindful step to move from fear to fiscal peace today.

My Journal Reflections

Spend at least five minutes in silent meditation each day for at least five days this week. Surrender your financial worries to God, then stop worrying about them. In these meditations, embrace the vulnerability of facing your financial worries and invite God's loving guidance into this area of your life. May His presence bring peace, wisdom, and a deeper understanding of His faithfulness in providing for your needs.

Day 1.   In your meditation, face your financial worries with honesty and vulnerability. Acknowledge the fears, anxieties, and uncertainties surrounding your financial situation. Surrender them to God, inviting His loving presence to bring peace and clarity to your financial concerns.

Day 2.   Focus your meditation on seeking God's guidance and wisdom in financial matters. Reflect on His role as the ultimate provider and ask for His divine guidance in managing your resources. Pray for discernment in making wise financial decisions aligned with His will.

Day 3.   Meditate on the topic of gratitude for the blessings in your financial life. Reflect on the ways God has provided for you in the past and express thankfulness for His faithfulness. Allow gratitude to fill your heart, shifting your focus from worries to the abundance and provision that God offers.

Day 4.   During your meditation, surrender the need to control and fixate on financial outcomes. Embrace the concept of stewardship, recognizing that everything you have is ultimately entrusted to you by God. Seek His guidance to manage your finances in alignment with His values and purposes.

Day 5.   Reflect on the topic of faith and trust in God's provision during your meditation. Contemplate the ways He has cared for you in the past and trust that He will continue to do so in the future. Pray for the strength to surrender financial worries, trusting in His divine plan and provision for your life.

CHAPTER 8

HARBORING RESENTMENT

Cease from anger and abandon wrath; Do not fret; it leads only to evil.

Psalm 37:8 Holman Christian Standard Bible

Six days after their last group-counseling session and one day before their next session, Brianna was still angry. For the entire week the only words spoken between her and her husband, Rashad, were necessary administrative comments like, "Did you remember to pick up the dry cleaning?"

As she braided her beautiful mane into cornrows for the night, Brianna tried to be present, but her mind kept returning to Rashad. Mentally, she fumed to God. She didn't want to go to the session. She felt so embarrassed and humiliated by what Rashad had said. He made it sound like for eighteen years, she had done nothing for him; she had been just a mother monster. How dare he!

The Takeaway

Sometimes we are so affronted by the words and actions of others that we can't see past it. This is especially true when those people are close to us, such as family members, coworkers, and friends.

During her morning meditations (yes, it took many sessions), Brianna's consultations with God led her to accept a few realities. The still small voice inside her yielded understanding. As much as she would like to, she couldn't control her husband's perspective on their marriage. She could only change her reactions, attitudes, and how she treated Rashad.

Brianna also reflected on her own behavior; the years she forgot their anniversary, the times she was too tired for intimacy after long days driving the kids around (even though Rashad was there too), how she snapped at him when she was tired (which was often), and how every sarcastic, denigrating comment she had made now stood between them like a moat of spikes, and she couldn't get through. No wonder he was filled with resentment!

Done with her hair, her long fingers drummed the dresser. She could see the negative patterns. "Dear God, can we fix this? I need your help." She whispered into the mirror.

My Journal Reflections

Start with a prayer then spend at least five minutes with God in silent meditation first thing each morning for at least five days this week. May these God-centered meditation prompts guide you in facing and releasing bitterness and resentment, allowing God's healing and grace to flow into your heart and relationships. May you find the freedom and peace that come from embracing forgiveness and cultivating a spirit of love and understanding.

Day 1.   During your meditation, courageously face any bitterness and resentment that may reside within your heart. Acknowledge the pain that these emotions have caused and the burden they have placed upon you. Surrender them to God's loving presence, seeking His healing and guidance in releasing these negative emotions.

Day 2.   Focus your meditation on the topic of forgiveness. Reflect on the power of God's forgiveness and His call to extend that forgiveness to others. Pray for the strength to let go of bitterness and resentment, allowing God's grace to soften your heart and bring healing to broken relationships.

Day 3.   Meditate on the topic of empathy and understanding. Reflect on the humanity and struggles of those who have caused you pain. Seek God's compassionate perspective, asking Him to help you see through His eyes and find compassion in your heart. Pray for the ability to release judgment and cultivate a spirit of empathy towards others.

Day 4.   Reflect on the transformative power of love during your meditation. Contemplate God's unconditional love and His ability to bring healing and reconciliation. Pray for the grace to let go of bitterness and embrace the transformative power of love, both in your relationship with God and with others.

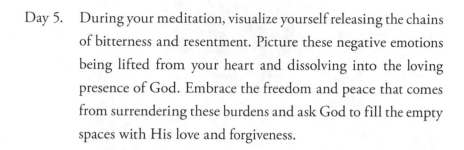

Day 5. During your meditation, visualize yourself releasing the chains of bitterness and resentment. Picture these negative emotions being lifted from your heart and dissolving into the loving presence of God. Embrace the freedom and peace that comes from surrendering these burdens and ask God to fill the empty spaces with His love and forgiveness.

CHAPTER 9
REJECT SELF-DOUBT

One whose mind remains undisturbed amidst misery, who does not crave for pleasure, and who is free from attachment, fear, and anger, is called a sage of steady wisdom.

Bhagavad Gita 2.56

As she did every Sunday evening, Singita faced her siblings on her computer screen. In birth order, Sarani, Salma, Sameena, and Bhakti, the youngest, looked back. The middle child, Singita, pulled her sisters together weekly.

"I don't understand why Appä disowned me. What was so wrong with me?" Singita asked.

"You mean why not Bhakti the tramp?" asked Sarani smacking on her mango, juice dribbling down her chubby chin.

"Hey!" Bhakti's black eyes blazed.

"Well, you did refuse to send him money and move to California to marry that wealthy Indian fellow. Screwing up Appä's immigration application was the last straw," Sarani said, nonplussed. "You weren't a very good girl now, were you? And there you sit, alone, unmarried, and unloved."

Singita's eyes burned with old fury. "I didn't refuse," she shot back, "I didn't have the money! And that guy was a waiter living in a slum. I didn't screw up Appä's immigration application. I even hired a lawyer, but it was denied!" She raged on. But secretly, Singita wondered about the truth in Sarani's biting remarks.

The Takeaway

Sometimes negative self-talk is so baked into our internal dialogues and enforced by those closest to us that we don't even notice it. Then over time, it becomes part of the normal wallpaper lining the halls of our minds, and we walk past it daily without even noticing how garish and ugly it is. And much of this negative self-talk is untrue.

We too readily accept the negative lies embedded in our minds about ourselves.

The purpose of meditation for God lovers is to centralize your practice upon God and reunite the soul with Him. It is in this reunification that

you can rediscover the divinity within you that is the reflection of God. You are created in his image. You hold his perfect goodness within you. In this moment you are the perfect combination of strengths, weaknesses, challenges and triumphs that have culminated in you being here right now.

Without blame, identify negative thought habits that have embedded themselves in your psyche. We often become what we think. Calling yourself unworthy, old, stupid, and so on, or accepting these labels from others, may become your reality.

Decide today not to give more space to the ugly thoughts.

My Journal Reflections

You didn't adopt your negative self-doubts in one sitting. Hence, it is important to affirm and reaffirm the truth over and over for a long period of time. Don't accept the first or even the second answer your brain throws at you for the lies you have accepted. Ask God to help you dig deep – there's more lurking back there. Start with five minutes but ruminate on this one and more will come to you. Keep coming back to these topics until you hear your new truths take root and raise their hands in your mind before the ugly stuff.

Day 1. In your meditation, bravely face the feelings of imposter syndrome and self-doubt. Acknowledge the insecurities and negative self-talk that may arise within you. Surrender these thoughts and emotions to God's loving presence, seeking His guidance and strength to overcome them.

Day 2.   Focus your meditation on the topic of embracing your true identity in God. Reflect on how He uniquely created you with purpose and intention. Pray for the ability to see yourself through His eyes, recognizing your inherent worth and the gifts He has bestowed upon you.

Day 3.   Meditate on the topic of self-compassion and self-acceptance. Reflect on God's unconditional love for you and His forgiveness for any mistakes or shortcomings. Pray for the grace to extend that same love and forgiveness to yourself, releasing the self-judgment and embracing a sense of worthiness.

Day 4.   Reflect on the topic of God's strength and empowerment within you during your meditation. Contemplate how His Spirit dwells within you, providing you with the confidence and ability to overcome self-doubt. Pray for His guidance to tap into this inner strength and live boldly according to His calling.

Day 5.   During your meditation, visualize yourself breaking free from the chains of imposter syndrome and self-doubt. Envision yourself stepping into your true identity as a beloved child of God, walking in confidence and purpose. Pray for the courage to trust in God's plan for your life and to live authentically without fear of judgment or comparison.

CHAPTER 10

CONFRONT ANXIETY

If only my grief could be weighed and my devastation placed with it in the scales. For then it would outweigh the sand of the seas! That is why my words are rash. Surely the arrows of the Almighty have pierced me; my spirit drinks their poison. God's terrors are arrayed against me.

Job 6: 1-4 Holman Christian Standard Bible

Brianna lay awake worrying about many things. Who was she without her children? Was Rashad right when he said all she had been the past eighteen years was a mother? Did she really treat her husband more like a utility player than a partner? Did she even want a partner? The last question snuck up on her, making her shudder as she mentally batted it away.

It was 2 o'clock in the morning, and Brianna and Rashad's children had only been gone a month. She was happy they were thriving and finding their way at college, and she couldn't do anything about their departure. She prayed and sat in meditation but didn't hear a response. But she could do something about her relationship with Rashad. She rolled over to face him as he lay snoring gently.

She used to love watching him sleep. But now, not even his distinguished gray temples or smooth caramel pores caught her attention. "Rashad, Rashad." He grunted and shifted. She put a hand on his arm. "Can we talk?" Rashad opened a single bleary eye and regarded her warily.

The Takeaway

Many of us are like Brianna. We lay awake at night, worries racing through our minds that balloon into giant fears with no solution. We worry about our jobs, our children, our relationships, the things we wish hadn't happened, and the things we are afraid will happen. Many of these worries are legitimate and we have valid reason to have concerns. But we also expend valuable time and energy that takes away from areas where we can better use that headspace. Sitting with God and pursuing a deeper relationship with him will naturally release many of the worries, fears, and anxieties that cause separation and cause interpersonal conflict.

Worries are like indecisive squirrels in the face of oncoming traffic. They run here and there with no direction and lead to no resolution.

Research shows that excessive worrying can have a negative impact on your relationships, sleep, job performance, and health.

One question to confront your anxiety is whether you can fix the subject of your worries right now. Do you have control over what's worrying you? If so, can you address it right this minute?

My Journal Reflections

This chapter is particularly helpful if you tend to 'catastrophize' with your thoughts running wild even when nothing scary is actually happening (like when you're lying in bed with no lions chasing you). Return to this chapter whenever you need to. Try not to think about the fact that you have worries. Breathe through them as you surrender them to God. Begin with a prayer and a few deep breaths. Then set your alarm for five minutes and meditate on a topic below for five minutes. Journal for greater clarity.

Day 1. In your meditation, courageously confront the habitual patterns of anxious thoughts that have held you captive. Recognize that these thoughts do not define you. Surrender them to God's loving presence, inviting Him to help you break free from their grip and replace them with His truth and peace.

Day 2. Focus your meditation on the topic of renewing your mind with God's Word. Reflect on Scripture passages that speak to overcoming anxiety and finding strength in God. Meditate on these verses, allowing them to reshape your thought patterns and replace anxious thoughts with God's promises.

Day 3. Meditate on the power of prayer in combating anxious thoughts. Embrace the practice of bringing your worries and concerns to God in prayer. Visualize yourself releasing each anxious thought into His hands, trusting Him to provide comfort, guidance, and peace in return.

Day 4.   Reflect on the topic of surrendering control and embracing God's sovereignty. During your meditation, release the need to control every outcome and acknowledge that God is in control of all things. Pray for the strength to surrender your anxious thoughts and trust in His perfect plan for your life.

Day 5.   Visualize yourself stepping out of the cycle of anxious thoughts and into the freedom of God's peace. See yourself walking hand-in-hand with Him, allowing His presence to guide you through each moment. Pray for the ability to recognize and let go of anxious thoughts as they arise, leaning on God's strength and trusting in His unfailing love.

CHAPTER 11
REPLACE ANXIETY

In this distress, — for then I had never had a single vision, — these Thy words alone were enough to remove it and give me perfect peace: 'Be not afraid, my daughter: it is I; and I will not abandon thee. Fear not.

St. Teresa of Avila

"I feel like we've drifted apart," Brianna began. Her husband said nothing. "I'd like to return to how things were when we started dating."

Rashad propped himself up on one elbow. "Oh, you mean back to the wonderful days when you got everything you wanted? When I ran behind you, always chasing and never satisfied? Back when I needed you more than you ever wanted me?" Brianna was taken aback. Rashad opened the floodgates. He was a brilliant engineer and had evidently catalogued everything he had ever been unhappy about in their marriage.

This wasn't how she envisioned this conversation going at all! There she was, trying to address a worry she could do something about like their support group leader, Cassie, taught them. But rather than alleviating her anxiety, her effort to confront the problem exacerbated it, adding a new beehive of stinging worries over the survival of her marriage.

The Takeaway

Life is imperfect. Sometimes the actions we take to address a problem seem to make it worse. Sometimes you might feel like God has a sense of humor and He's laughing at your predicament. It doesn't mean the original intent was wrong. But as in Brianna's case, people and situations can react in unexpected ways.

Rather than allowing unexpected twists to add to your anxiety, you can still replace the worry habit. Habits of thought are more powerful than habits of behavior because:

First we think, then we do, then we become.

Changing thought habits is incredibly difficult in part because thoughts travel down well-defined neural pathways that grow stronger with repetition, just like your physical muscles grow stronger with exercise. So rather than gritting your teeth and trying to muscle your way out of a negative thought habit, it may be easier to simply focus on replacing the worry thought habit with a new habit. Ask for God's

help during your morning meditation time and spend a few focused minutes confronting your negative thoughts and practicing replacing each thought with the positive message with which you want to replace it. It will get easier with time.

My Journal Reflections

Get serious about defeating your negative thought-habits no matter how long it takes and however many times you need to return to these reflections. You can do all things through God who strengthens you and He can show you how to defeat this stronghold. Lean into His guidance. May God's truth, promises, and presence guide you in cultivating a mindset rooted in His love, peace, and faith. Begin with a prayer and a few deep breaths. Then set your alarm for five minutes and meditate on a topic below for five minutes. Journal for greater clarity.

Day 1.   In your meditation, become aware of anxious thoughts as they arise. Take a moment to pause and consciously choose to replace them with positive and empowering thoughts rooted in God's truth. Focus on affirmations such as "I am held in God's love and peace" or "I trust in His perfect plan for me."

Day 2.   Reflect on the topic of gratitude during your meditation. Shift your attention from anxious thoughts to the blessings in your life. Engage in a practice of gratitude by focusing on the goodness of God and expressing thankfulness for His provision, guidance, and love. Allow gratitude to replace anxious thoughts with a sense of joy and contentment.

Day 3.   Meditate on the promises of God's faithfulness and provision. As anxious thoughts emerge, consciously bring to mind His promises, such as "God is with me always" or "He will never leave nor forsake me." Repeat these promises as affirmations, allowing them to instill confidence and trust, replacing anxious thoughts with a deep sense of peace.

Day 4.   Reflect on the power of prayer in transforming anxious thoughts. During your meditation, bring your concerns to God in prayer, releasing them into His hands. As you surrender these worries, replace them with prayers of trust, surrender, and faith. Embrace the assurance that God hears your prayers and will guide you through any challenging circumstances.

Day 5.   Visualize a positive and empowering future during your meditation. Imagine yourself stepping into the life that God has planned for you, filled with purpose, joy, and peace. Replace anxious thoughts with visions of success, love, and fulfillment. Embrace the truth that with God's guidance and strength, you can overcome challenges and live a life of abundance.

CHAPTER 12

OVERCOME IMPOSTER SYNDROME

One who remains unattached under all conditions, and is neither delighted by good fortune nor dejected by tribulation, he is a sage with perfect knowledge.

Bhagavad Gita 2.57

Singita was frustrated. All day a single thought had been tormenting her like an irrepressible demon, riding her shoulders, *I am not enough. Appä knows it, and my sisters do too.* Over multiple meditative reflections, she realized she had been carrying this lie since childhood. It was so embedded in her psyche that she never questioned or even recognized it was there. It took a lot of introspection and going step-by-step through her personal history to identify times when that thought rooted itself more deeply or when it influenced her outward behavior.

In frustration she plopped down on her meditation pillow in a corner of her tiny but sunny apartment, closed her eyes, and angrily said aloud, "God, I'm so tired of carrying this around!" Mentally she yelled at her tormenting thoughts "Step into the light and tell God what you've been saying to me all day!" She hadn't expected a result, but she immediately felt a tingling sensation and the sense of a weight being lifted from her shoulders. In her mind's eye she saw the words *You are not enough* emblazoned across a vast blue sky. As she watched, the words shrank and shrank until they were scratched on a little posterboard behind which the head and most of a knobby-kneed sharp angled creature hid. As if discovered, the creature trembled. A spotlight blazed on with a brilliant light more blindingly white than she had ever seen. But it didn't hurt. Like a roach, the creature crept away with its pathetic sign.

Singita marveled at how the roaring lie that had weighed her down like an anvil was reduced to no more than a pathetic squeak. Talking to God really worked, she thought. Why didn't she do this earlier? She understood that the origin of this lie didn't reside in any single event but in statements and insinuations from family members that were compounded with her own insecurities. It didn't happen in a day or even a month. But over time and with iterative practice, Singita grew strong enough to banish the lie consistently, with longer and longer periods between its return. On increasingly rare occasions, she still must wrestle it to the ground when it comes slinking back unnoticed.

The Takeaway

Too often when we are called to fill the void of another's unexplained intentions, we immediately migrate toward the negative. Then we use our internal dialogue to give the negative statements life and breath.

Be kind to yourself regarding what could be only the tip of an iceberg you didn't even know was there. To catch yourself in negative self-talk, you can take a simple step like wearing a rubber band around your wrist. Snap it each time you hear yourself say something ugly to yourself. Then you must intentionally redirect your thoughts to a positive replacement thought. Consult a professional if necessary to help you uproot the weeds of deep-seated negative thoughts. Sometimes the prisons we construct in our minds are more powerful than any walls outside of ourselves.

My Journal Reflections

This week's meditation topics may require you to reflect deeply and return to these topics repeatedly. That's okay; as long as there is breath in your body, there is opportunity to take another step toward loving yourself. As you pray, ask God to show you…so much. Then set your alarm for five minutes and meditate on a topic below for five minutes. Journal for greater clarity.

Day 1.   In your meditation, courageously confront the negative self-talk that fuels your imposter syndrome. Recognize that these thoughts are not your true identity. Invite God's loving presence to reveal the lies you have embraced and replace them with His truth and affirmations of your worth and purpose. How do these lies drive your behaviors?

Day 2.   Focus your meditation on the topic of embracing God's perspective of you. Reflect on how He sees you as His beloved child, fearfully and wonderfully made. Pray for His guidance in identifying the negative lies that hinder your confidence and ask Him to replace them with His truth about who you are in Him. What did you learn?

Day 3. Meditate on the power of God's unconditional love. Reflect on His relentless pursuit of your heart and His acceptance of you as you are. Allow His love to penetrate the lies that have held you captive, replacing them with the truth that you are deeply loved and valued by Him.

Day 4. Reflect on the topic of your unique purpose and calling. During your meditation, ask God to reveal the gifts and talents He has bestowed upon you. Embrace the truth that you have been uniquely created and equipped for a specific purpose. Replace the negative lies with affirmations of your divine calling and the impact you can make in the world. How would your life change if you embraced healthy new truths about yourself?

Day 5. Visualize yourself uprooting the negative lies that fuel your imposter syndrome. Picture yourself digging deep into the soil of your heart, pulling out each lie with the strength and guidance of God. As you remove the lies, envision your heart being filled with God's truth and affirmations of your identity in Him.

CHAPTER 13

DON'T MIND ALTER

Don't you know that your body is a sanctuary of the Holy Spirit who is in you, whom you have from God? You are not your own, for you were bought at a price. Therefore, glorify God in your body.

1 Corinthians 6:19-20 Holman Christian Standard Bible

Rashad studied the pills in his hand. They beckoned like whispers in the trees. Mentally, he explained his situation to God. He didn't want to die, just to sleep for a week. Or maybe until the tension with Bri ended. How long could you sleep with enough dosage and still live? He was so tired of the angry silence that lurked in every room of their home. His anger and desire to leave the marriage were supposed to punish her, but they were choking him. Rolling the pills in his hand, he faced a certain truth: He hated his life.

Bitterness is like drinking poison and waiting for the other person to die.

The Takeaway

Your body is a physical temple in which your consciousness resides. We only get one temple. It is precious and irreplaceable. If injured badly enough, no amount of money can restore it.

In the dark season, it may be tempting to separate your temple from your consciousness. What you are going through might be so painful that this separation seems like a real option. It is not.

God doesn't issue orders to make your life difficult. There are always loving reasons behind His edicts. The spiritual reason to honor your temple is clear. But there are other practical reasons to honor your temple. No good comes from taking mind-altering substances that cause you to lose consciousness beyond the kind of assistance that over the counter or medically prescribed medications provide. Leaving your temple unattended can result in many dangerous consequences: Your body may fall into the hands of predators who would harm you; you may be permanently damaged; in a blacked-out state, you may say or do things you'll regret later. Worst of all, you may not be able to wake up. Whatever bad season you are running away from, drinking, or drugging yourself to oblivion is bound to make everything worse. The emotional

pain may be excruciating at its peak, but just remember it is darkest before dawn breaks.

Ask God for help to maintain the integrity of your temple. Then look with confident expectation for signs of help, which may come in the form of individuals in your life who show up with just the right expertise that you need. Talk to a professional or join a support group if you need to. If in the United States, you can access immediate help in English or Spanish on the suicide hotline by dialing 988 for help. Persevere. Choose to endure your season of tribulation with your consciousness intact. Yes, you can do it!

My Journal Reflections

Start with a prayer then spend at least five minutes with God in silent meditation each day for at least 5 days this week. Resist mind altering as much as possible. Seek professional help if you need it. May these God-centered meditation prompts encourage you to abandon thoughts and temptations to rely on mind-altering substances during difficult times. May God's presence, peace, and guidance be your source of strength and solace. May you find healthier and more sustainable ways to cope with challenges, leaning on His love and support.

Day 1.   In your meditation, acknowledge any thoughts or temptations to turn to mind-altering substances during difficult times. Surrender these thoughts to God's loving presence, recognizing that He offers comfort, strength, and guidance in the midst of challenges. Pray for His wisdom and support to overcome these temptations and find healthier ways to cope.

Day 2.   Focus your meditation on the topic of seeking God's peace
         and solace in difficult times. Reflect on the truth that God is a
         refuge and source of comfort. Visualize yourself resting in His
         loving embrace, finding solace and strength in His presence.
         Pray for His grace to help you resist the allure of mind-altering
         substances and rely on His peace instead.

Day 3.   Meditate on the power of prayer as a tool to navigate difficult
         times. Rather than seeking an escape through mind-altering
         substances, invite God into your struggles through prayer.
         Allow His presence and guidance to provide you with the
         strength and resilience needed to face challenges head-on. Pray
         for His intervention and support during difficult moments.

Day 4.   Reflect on the topic of self-care and healthy coping mechanisms
         during your meditation. Consider alternative ways to address
         stress and difficulties in your life, such as engaging in physical
         activity, seeking support from loved ones, or pursuing creative
         outlets. Pray for God's guidance in finding healthy and
         constructive ways to navigate challenging times.

Day 5.   Visualize yourself empowered by God's strength to overcome
         temptations and negative thoughts. See yourself equipped with
         His armor of truth, protecting you from the lure of mind-
         altering substances. Pray for His protection and resolve to resist
         the temptation, knowing that He will provide the strength to
         persevere.

CHAPTER 14

ACKNOWLEDGE HURT

May the Lord reward you for what you have done, and
may you receive a full reward from the Lord God of Israel,
under whose wings you have come for refuge.

Ruth 2:12 Holman Christian Standard Bible

That night, Rashad had a dream in which he was wading through life as if mired in molasses. God didn't speak in a voice, but Rashad understood that the pills would risk permanent impairment. When he woke, he understood the warning and ultimately decided against the pills. But he still had to sort through his anger and resentment toward Bri. During his meditation time, he worked on the assignment Cassie had given the class. "An early step in the journey to healing is acknowledging the hurt you suffered. Sometimes we carry it around, nurse it, allow it to take over parts of our lives without ever truly expressing it. Sometimes we don't want to let it go," she'd said.

He started with five minutes in the morning but found himself ruminating on the topic throughout the day. He had been praying about his marriage, and Rashad knew he had to face the reasons he was holding on to his anger. At first, he hid it from God, but once he realized that God already knew what he was running from, he opened himself up during his meditation sessions. Over time, he uncovered several reasons he continued to cling to his anger. In the safety of his heavenly Father's loving arms, he gained the bravery to view his motivations honestly and without judgment, which allowed him to fully acknowledge them. He was afraid that letting his anger go would condone Bri's hurtful behavior. His anger created a protective shell around his heart. Relinquishing it would open him up to old hurts. He enjoyed treating Bri as if he didn't need her; it made him feel powerful. He also liked being the victim, the wronged. His bitterness was revenge. He didn't know who he would be without his resentment. Letting it go might signal the true end of their relationship.

The Takeaway

Whatever your reasons, it can take a very long time to even acknowledge the depth of pain you have suffered. Today's reflection is just a first step. It might take years to heal but start by fully acknowledging the hurt that was done to you.

> *It's much easier to be angry than admit hurt. But hurt is often the primary emotion masked behind the anger.*

If you have been carrying the hurt around for decades, mentally go back to the age you were when the hurt happened and address the hurt that child experienced.

My Journal Reflections

Start with a prayer then spend at least five minutes with God in silent meditation each morning for at least five days this week. This chapter can take hours and years to fully unpack. Be patient with yourself and stay with it until you really know in your soul that you have let go of the hurts. Ask God to test your heart and show you any dark corners that remain. Then work on it some more.

Day 1.   In your meditation, bravely acknowledge the hurt caused by others in your life. Allow yourself to feel the pain and disappointment without judgment. Surrender these emotions to God's loving presence, inviting His healing and guidance as you seek to move past the hurt.

Day 2.   Focus your meditation on the topic of forgiveness. Reflect on God's grace and His call to extend forgiveness to those who have hurt you. Pray for the strength to release any resentment or bitterness, recognizing that forgiveness is a gift you give yourself. Ask God to help you let go of the hurt and embrace a spirit of compassion and reconciliation.

Day 3.   Meditate on the power of empathy and understanding. Reflect on the humanness of others, recognizing that their actions may have stemmed from their own pain or brokenness. Pray for the ability to see beyond the hurtful actions and to foster a spirit of empathy, allowing God's love to heal both you and those who have caused you pain.

Day 4.   Reflect on the topic of surrendering the desire for justice and revenge. During your meditation, release the need for vindication and trust in God's ultimate justice. Pray for His guidance in embracing a mindset of grace and mercy, knowing that He is the ultimate judge and will right every wrong in His perfect timing.

Day 5.   Visualize yourself releasing the grip of hurt and pain during your meditation. Picture your heart opening up to God's healing presence, allowing His love to fill the spaces once occupied by hurt. Pray for the strength to let go of the past and embrace a future marked by growth, forgiveness, and the restoration of relationships.

CHAPTER 15

WORRY FAST

Cassie's smile was benevolent. "A worry fast is making the choice to
quit worrying cold turkey for some period." Shadow The Cat slid under
Singita's dangling feet, enjoying the inadvertent stroking. Singita kicked
him in the ribs, making him hiss and flash his one good eye angrily at
her before slinking off. Brianna suppressed a grin while Barry scowled.
Cassie continued. "Obviously the ideal is that you are on a permanent

worry fast. But for most of us, that is very difficult if not impossible to achieve." She let that sink in.

"Purposefully surrender your worries to God and consciously choose to fast between certain times." Cassie taught them a meditation technique that involved visualizing their worries traveling from their brains down their arms and out into their open palms. There they mentally wrapped the worries in gift boxes and watched them float up to God like helium balloons. For example, release your worries for the first hour of your day. Over lunch, simply enjoy being in the present moment, and don't allow your mind to race. Remember that most of the things you worry about aren't actually happening at the time you're worrying about them."

Events are not the cause of your stress. Your thoughts about past or potential events (many of which may not happen) are the cause of your stress. Tame your stress by taming your mind.

Cassie peered around the room. Shadow The Cat slithered around Rashad's ankles, but he didn't notice. "When you get home at night, decide not to allow that cantankerous spouse or those nagging parents to worry you no matter how vexatious they are." She gestured broadly. "The next day don't worry about your progress! Just pick up from where you left off the previous day. Whenever you catch those worries nagging you again, practice the same visualization technique and relinquish them to God. For many of us, worrying is a negative thought habit, so expect to practice this technique as often as necessary."

The Takeaway

Quelling anxiety is a choice. Your mind won't settle down by itself. You need to *decide* to stop worrying and take active steps to make that happen. One shortcut is to cast your cares on God. Cassie shared one technique, but you can do this in whatever way feels right for you.

Identifying the aspects of a problem you can control may reveal that there's nothing about it that you can, in fact, control. If you cannot control the problem, once you surrender it to God, decide to stop worrying about it because your worry won't change the outcome. And don't worry if this doesn't work the first time you try. As long as there is breath in your body, there is another opportunity to try. Keep releasing the gift boxes to God whenever you find that you've recaptured them.

My Journal Reflections

Most of us think of trials and struggles as "bad". But in many cases, they present rich opportunities for personal growth and strength. Can you accept the challenges that come your way without judging them as bad and reacting to them in kind? Begin with a prayer and a few deep breaths. Then set your alarm for five minutes and meditate on a topic below for five minutes. Journal for greater clarity.

Day 1. During your meditation, commit to a short worry fast at a specific time of the day. Choose a time that works best for you, such as the morning or before bedtime. Surrender your worries to God's loving care during this designated period, knowing that He is in control. Embrace the peace that comes from releasing your concerns and allowing His presence to bring calm to your mind.

Day 2.   Mentally expand your worry fast in your meditation, selecting a slightly longer period later in the day to abstain from worrying. Use this time to consciously choose trust over worry, inviting God's peace to fill your heart. Pray for His strength to resist the urge to worry and to lean on His faithfulness. Replace anxious thoughts with thoughts of renewal and rejuvenation, trusting that God will provide and guide you through any challenges.

Day 3.   In today's meditation, visualize yourself extending the time period of your worry fast to a longer period than yesterday. Set aside this specific time to pause, release your worries to Him like helium balloons, and trust in God's provision. Pray for His grace to help you let go of anxious thoughts and embrace His peace. Use these five minutes to connect with God, seeking His guidance and wisdom in all areas of your life.

Day 4.   Meditate on the idea of a worry fast to a different time of day than you have used in previous days. Choose a specific time to dedicate to releasing your concerns and embracing God's peace before the day comes to a close. Pray for His strength to surrender your worries and find rest in His presence. Allow this worry-free time to be a time of reflection, gratitude, and trust, knowing that God is faithful to carry your burdens.

Day 5.   Select a specific time in the morning to release your worries to God and invite His peace into your day. Pray for His guidance and strength to let go of anxious thoughts and trust in His provision. Use your meditation time to set a positive and peaceful tone for the day ahead, knowing that God is with you every step of the way.

CHAPTER 16

PRACTICE FORGIVENESS

Do not take revenge or bear a grudge against members of your community, but love your neighbor as yourself; I am Yahweh.
Leviticus 19:18 Holman Christian Standard Bible

"This forgiveness thing takes forever," Barry said, chugging his black coffee after their workout. "The seventh step of AA involves asking our Higher Power to remove our shortcomings. Essentially, I had to ask for forgiveness for all the crap I'd done. But forgiving someone else," he shook his head. "That's somethin' else."

Rashad took a sip of water. "I hear you, man. Every day I spend my meditation time fighting to forgive her. I want to be angry."

Barry nodded. "I get it," he said. He looked around Rashad's pale-green man cave. The swanky shed was lined with shelves boasting obsessively tidy rows of more computer gadgetry than Barry could name. Rashad, a software engineer, had found ways to fill all the time his wife left him alone over the years.

"Holdin' that anger will lead you down my road. In my case, it was my father-in-law's anger but same difference; I'm divorced from the love of my life, drownin' in child support, missin' my kids like crazy, and wonderin' why all our friends went with her. Ironically, he thinks he won his daughter back. But I know her. She's miserable. His anger and hate destroyed all our lives."

Rashad studied Barry and then said, "Our kids are in college so …"

Barry waved, dismissively. "Right. But the rest is true. Divorce is awful. You don't wanna go there."

"But you're free! All options open." Rashad was envious.

"To do what, Rashad?" Barry asked. "Go partyin'? Sleep around? Start drinkin' again? Do you really want that life?" Rashad couldn't relate to the drinking part, but he shook his head as he considered.

Barry said, "Decide if you want your marriage and then stay or go. But don't do this." Barry waved figure eights at his friend. "You won't be able to fully engage in your marriage if you don't forgive her." Rashad stared through the large window he had cut into the side of the shed and twisted his mouth to the side. "Aside from God forgiving you to the extent that you forgive her, it will free you to truly enjoy your marriage."

The Takeaway

Barry's is a cautionary tale. Avoid the hard road if possible. It might take years of repeated practice to fully forgive. It's hard.

Forgiveness isn't condoning the other's behavior. It's unshackling yourself so you can move forward. Forgive, even if the other doesn't deserve it. Carrying resentment and bitterness will harm *your* mind and body.

Decide today not to allow your past to hold your future prisoner.

My Journal Reflections

Start with a prayer then spend at least five minutes with God in silent meditation first thing each morning for at least 5 days this week. This one isn't easy; it's hard. Keep at it.

Day 1.   In your meditation, bravely explore how your pain is affecting you. Reflect on the ways it holds you back, limits your growth, or hinders your well-being. Surrender these effects to God's loving presence, asking for the courage to let go and release the grip of pain on your life.

Day 2.   Focus your meditation on the topic of healing and restoration. Reflect on the possibilities that lie beyond your pain and the freedom that comes from letting go. Pray for God's guidance and strength to release the hold of pain, trusting in His transformative power to bring healing and wholeness.

Day 3.   Meditate on the topic of forgiveness, both for others and for yourself. Reflect on the ways that holding onto pain and resentment can perpetuate harm. Pray for the grace to forgive those who have hurt you and to release any self-blame or guilt.

Ask God to help you find the courage to let go of the pain and embrace a path of healing and forgiveness.

Day 4.   Reflect on the topic of surrender during your meditation. Contemplate the idea of releasing your pain into God's loving hands, trusting that He can carry it and bring beauty from ashes. Pray for the strength to surrender your pain, relinquishing control and opening yourself up to His healing and transformative work.

Day 5.   Visualize yourself releasing the chains of pain during your meditation. Picture the weight and burden being lifted off your shoulders, allowing God's love and light to fill the space once occupied by pain. Pray for the courage to let go, embracing the freedom and peace that come from releasing the hold of pain and stepping into a new chapter of healing and growth.

CHAPTER 17
OVERCOME LOSS

Do not take revenge or bear a grudge against members of your community, but love your neighbor as yourself; I am Yahweh.

Psalm 34:8 Holman Christian Standard Bible

"So, what's the story with your dad?" Brianna asked Singita as they left a session. Singita was a petite bouncing splash of red and yellow next to her statuesque companion gliding in muted shades of gold and orange.

Singita sighed. "Appä beat us all except for my youngest sister, Bhakti. My sisters resent her for that." Singita explained her dad's demands for more money than she made, "He thinks that since I live in America, I must be rich." She cackled derisively. After she failed to pay him, refused to marry the stranger who was the son of a great Indian family, and his immigration application was denied, her dad declared Singita dead to him. "He even had a funeral at home in India, so we can never reconcile. And he still uses Ammä to ask for money." Singita hung her head, filled with regrets.

"You need to do what I need to do, Singita," Brianna said. "Accept what's gone. Stop chasing after what you don't have and what you lost. Make peace with it. Accept your past and the fact that your dad could not have been any different. Then inventory what you do have and move forward in appreciation of that." Brianna explained how she had leaned on God to help her release her resentments. "That technique of releasing my resentments to God in gift boxes like helium balloons really worked. It was slow going at first and I kept having to repeat it. But now I have longer periods of peace," she said. Slowly but surely, it was working. Singita countered by sharing that she had a difficult time envisioning a loving Father God, given the terrible earthly example she had endured.

The Takeaway

Studies have shown that human beings are often more motivated by loss than by what can be gained or even what they have. Singita flowed in the river of negativity that her father created for them both. Even though she couldn't change his ways, she still felt regret and guilt. This relationship influences how Singita treats and views relationships in every aspect of her life. She mourns not just for the father she has but for the one she wishes she had. Acceptance and forgiveness are key parts of healing these kinds of rifts.

My Journal Reflections

If you have been focused on what you have lost, let today be the first day you shift your focus to what you have and have gained. Perhaps the loss of that toxic relationship paved the way for harmony and healing. Begin with a prayer and a few deep breaths. Then set your alarm for five minutes and meditate on a topic below for five minutes. Journal for greater clarity. Your journaling may be especially helpful in charting your plan.

Day 1. In your meditation, acknowledge the personal losses you have experienced. Reflect on the pain and grief associated with these losses. Surrender them to God's loving presence, seeking His comfort and guidance as you navigate the process of healing and finding new meaning in the midst of loss.

Day 2. For today's five minutes, focus your meditation on the topic of God's faithfulness and provision. Reflect on how He has carried you through past losses and brought you to where you are today. Pray for the strength and trust to lean on His unfailing love and guidance as you overcome personal losses, knowing that He will provide for your needs and bring restoration.

Day 3. Meditate on the topic of surrendering the need for control and finding peace in God's plan. Reflect on the truth that God works all things together for good, even in the face of personal losses. Pray for the grace to release your expectations and trust in His divine wisdom, knowing that He will bring beauty from ashes.

Day 4.   Reflect on the topic of finding hope and purpose in the midst of personal losses during your meditation. Contemplate the ways God can use your experiences to shape and strengthen you. Pray for the courage to embrace new opportunities and allow your losses to become stepping stones towards a deeper understanding of God's plan for your life.

Day 5.   Visualize yourself stepping forward into a future filled with God's restoration and joy. During your meditation, picture yourself releasing the weight of personal losses and embracing the new possibilities that lie ahead. Pray for the strength to let go of the past and walk forward in faith, knowing that God is with you every step of the way.

CHAPTER 18

WHY MEDITATE WHEN I ATTEND CHURCH OR TEMPLE

May my meditation be pleasing to Him; I will rejoice in the Lord.

Psalm 104:34 Holman Christian Standard Bible

"I got a dumb question", Barry blurted out as he scratched his inner thigh.

"There's no such thing," Cassie declared without missing a beat.

"Hmmm, I don't know," Singita mused, throwing Barry a side eye.

Leaning forward, Barry rested his elbows on his thighs. Looking earnest and confused, he said, "At AA I learned to surrender to my Higher Power. Do I even need this meditation stuff?"

"I attend a church. Do I need it?" inquired Brianna.

"I go to temple. What about me?" Singita chimed in.

Cassie nodded with each question. "Well, it's like this," she began. "Imagine that your Divine Mother lives in this place you call church." She paused and winked at Singita saying, "It's a bit easier for you at temple since there's more opportunity for unstructured prayer and meditation time, right?"

Singita nodded, heavy ponytail bobbing.

Cassie turned to the rest of the group. "Okay. So, it's Sunday morning, you go to your Divine Mother's house and park in a pew. Closing your eyes you say, "Hi Ma…" Immediately somebody leaps onto the stage and invites you to sing about how wonderful your mom is."

Barry scowled. Confusion reflected in the faces around the circle. Cassie continued nonplussed.

"So everyone stands up and sings. When you sit, you close your eyes, "Hi Ma." Just then, someone begins announcements for what's happening in and around your mother's house."

Light dawned in Barry's eyes.

Cassie continued, "After announcements, you try again, but here's the cute children's performance. Eventually, the pastor takes the stage. When he asks you to close your eyes, he talks to your mom for you with words from his heart while you listen. They're good words, but not your words."

Next to Singita, Brianna was nodding.

"The pastor tells you all about your mom, her love, her actions, and her teachings. Before you know it, service is over, you are dismissed from your mom's house, and you never got a chance to talk to her."

The Takeaway

Cassie isn't knocking conventional worship, but making an important distinction.

Attending meetings with a coworker with no one-on-one time, doesn't build a friendship.

Combining communal worship and personal meditation can intertwine into the optimal, spiritual walk. Places of worship can yield significant benefits in learning and building like-minded community. Meditation, whether alone or in a group, creates inward space for dialogue with the Divine.

My Journal Reflections

Absolutely seek out others to strengthen your walk with God. But also make time for solitary communion in the same way that you might set aside personal time to build a friendship with a coworker. This week, plan to do both. Begin with a prayer and a few deep breaths. Then set your alarm for five minutes and meditate on a topic below for five minutes. Journal for greater clarity.

Day 1.　During your five-minute meditation, focus on the goodness and beauty of the practice itself. Reflect on how it feels to be still in the presence of God, allowing His peace and love to wash over you. Embrace the unique experience of connecting with God through meditation and savor the moments of stillness and tranquility.

Day 2.   Meditate on the topic of deeper introspection and self-awareness. Explore how the practice of meditation allows you to go beyond words and connect with God on a profound level. Reflect on the ways in which meditation provides an opportunity for quiet reflection and deepening your understanding of yourself and your relationship with God.

Day 3.   For the next five minutes, reflect on the unique benefits of meditation as compared to prayer. During your meditation, contemplate how the practice allows you to quiet your mind, let go of distractions, and simply be in the presence of God. Explore how it differs from talking to God in prayer, as it offers a space for receiving, listening, and being fully present with Him.

Day 4.   Meditate on the topic of surrender and receptivity. Reflect on how the practice of meditation enables you to let go of your own thoughts, desires, and agendas, allowing God's presence to fill your mind and heart. Pray for the grace to be open and receptive to God's guidance, wisdom, and love during your meditation practice.

Day 5.   Visualize yourself experiencing the transformative power of meditation during your practice. Picture the light of God's presence illuminating your inner being, bringing clarity, peace, and renewal. Pray for the ability to fully embrace the practice of meditation and its unique ability to connect you with God in a profound and transformative way.

DAWN

The Significance of Dawn

I rise to the brilliant sun beyond the dark ravine.

Dawn is a season of new beginnings:

- A new job, new school, new town you just settled in.
- A new baby or family member.
- A new day full of possibilities.
- The beginning of a new week.

In the season of Dawn, as the sun rises upon the horizon, we are reminded of the eternal truth that hope and deliverance can emerge even from the darkest of nights. Just as the world awakens to a new day, we too can find a renewed sense of purpose and divine intervention in our lives. It is in this tranquil moment of mindfulness that we open ourselves to the presence of God, allowing His light to illuminate our paths and guide us towards a future filled with promise.

As we embrace the gentle stillness of the dawn, we recognize that God's mercy and grace are not bound by time or circumstance. In this sacred connection, we find solace and strength, trusting that His love can bring healing and restoration to our weary souls. So, let us immerse ourselves in the beauty of Dawn, knowing that in this season of new beginnings, God's hope and deliverance are ever-present, ready to transform our lives.

Maximizing your success in this season of newness includes mindfully planning for new opportunities with hope and optimism.

CHAPTER 1

DON'T PANIC

Cast your burden on the Lord, and He will sustain you; He will never allow the righteous to be shaken.
Psalm 55:22 Holman Christian Standard Bible

Singita Patel is late! She is watching her sister's three kids for the week while Salma and her husband are on vacation. She leaps from bed and flies around the house like a rogue basketball player with spiked platform stilts and a frenetic ponytail. She rounds up kids, backpacks, and lunchboxes. No bread means she can't make sandwiches. The kids have only one gear—tortoise—so they lollygag.

"I need $20 for today's field trip," chirps her nephew as she screeches into the school parking lot. She has no cash. And her day is just beginning. Aaaaarrrrrrgggggghhhhh!

Across town, Barry Miles is also running late. He calmly trims his red buzz cut. Then he takes five minutes to sit down in his meditation chair and calm himself. He begins with a prayer. "Dear God, I'm running late. Please help me." In sitting with God, he takes calming breaths. He accepts he is running late and can't reclaim that time. During his five minutes, he mentally maps out what he needs to do to adjust. The last time he didn't take time for himself, he passed out on a plane and almost lost five-year-old Navesh, who was rescued by another passenger. The flight landed safely, but it was a frightening wake-up call. Now, in his five minutes of reflection, he even considers what to say to his tortoises, Naveen and Navesh, to motivate them to crawl faster.

Once on the road, he silently curses the traffic jam, so his chirpy sons don't hear. Even then, he mentally reroutes his day to accommodate the additional delay.

The Takeaway

We all have hectic days. It is counterintuitive to take five extra minutes when you're already behind. Panicking won't help but taking five minutes to collect yourself will. Each time you face a situation you can't control, first pause, and take a calming breath. Try and connect to God's presence within you. Anchor yourself to that peace that stands unshaken and unwavering through even the most turbulent situation. Acknowledge what you can't control and then adapt to the situation.

My Journal Reflections

Start with a prayer then spend at least five minutes with God in silent meditation before you fly into a panic. May these God-centered meditation prompts inspire you to pause and find calmness in the midst of panic, frustration, or flustered feelings. May God's presence and peace fill your heart as you take five minutes to center yourself, seeking His guidance and surrendering control. May you experience the transformative power of finding calmness in His loving embrace.

Day 1.　In your meditation, embrace the opportunity to pause and find calmness when feelings of panic, frustration, or fluster arise. Surrender these emotions to God's loving presence, inviting His peace to wash over you. Take five minutes to focus on deep breathing and allow His soothing presence to restore your inner tranquility.

Day 2.　Focus your meditation on the topic of surrendering control and finding peace in God's presence. When you feel overwhelmed, take five minutes to pause and release your worries, anxieties, and frustrations to Him. Pray for His guidance and strength to navigate the situation with grace and peace, knowing that He is in control.

Day 3.　Meditate on the power of gratitude and perspective during your five-minute calming practice. Shift your focus from the immediate stressors to the blessings and goodness in your life. Take a few moments to express gratitude to God for His presence, provision, and unwavering love. Allow gratitude to reshape your perspective and bring a sense of calm and gratitude.

Day 4.   Reflect on the topic of trust in God's timing and plan. When faced with frustration or impatience, take five minutes to center yourself in His presence. Pray for the grace to trust that He is working all things for your good and His perfect timing. Release the need for immediate solutions and find peace in knowing that He is guiding your steps.

Day 5.   Visualize a calming and peaceful scene during your meditation. Close your eyes and imagine yourself in a serene environment, such as a tranquil garden or by the still waters. Take five minutes to immerse yourself in this visualization, allowing God's peace to wash over you and replenish your spirit.

CHAPTER 2

CHOOSE DAWN

For I know the plans I have for you"—this is the Lord's declaration—"plans for your welfare, not for disaster, to give you a future and a hope.
Jeremiah 29:11 Holman Christian Standard Bible

"Today we are going to choose our dawn." Cassie smoothed her mud-brown skirt and surveyed the group.

"What d'ya mean?" asked Barry, his gray eyes clouding with suspicion. He cuddled Shadow The Cat in a burly embrace, vigorously scratching his good ear, while the cat seemed to contemplate whether to stay or escape.

Cassie gestured toward him. Her posture and movement made him think of a princess turned hunched young witch. Except during meditation, she always seemed to fold in on herself to be smaller. She said, "Well you're a perfect example, Barry. You're divorced now, right?"

He shifted. "Well yeah," he said. "But you said it could take the next five years to recover from my ten-year marriage."

Cassie nodded. "That's true. But now you can live your dawns. You're not going to be well in a flash; it's an iterative process."

Cassie turned to Rashad and Brianna. "Your children are gone. Time has thrust dawn upon you, but it's up to you to make it wonderful." The couple looked at each other dubiously. "Or you can choose to remain in the dark season. The choice is yours."

The Takeaway

It is your attitude and choice, not circumstance, that define your Dawn.

Although dawn can break in your life with a big life-changing event like a new baby, a new spouse, a new home, or a new job, it can also creep in like the sunrise. When it comes, you can choose to greet God with joy, bound out of bed and bask in the glow of the rising sun, or you can dive into the dark under your blankets and hide from the glorious rays.

Dawn can be triggered by an event. But more often, it can be a choice. No matter what has happened in your life today, you can choose dawn. The Bible says *fear not* or some form of the admonition not to fear, 365 times. That's one assurance for each day of the year. What if you lived each day without fear? What if you embrace God's light each day and show up with courage and exuberance no matter what?

My Journal Reflections

God actually gives you great latitude to choose your destiny and daily actions. He's not waiting to judge or punish you for your choices – even the ones that yield negative consequences (you essentially punish yourself through those negative consequences). Even if your season doesn't feel fully like dawn, consider whether you can choose dawn today. Ask God to show you the way. He'll help you along the way. Begin with a prayer and a few deep breaths. Then set your alarm for five minutes and meditate on a topic below for five minutes. Journal for greater clarity.

Day 1.   In today's five-minute meditation, embrace the choice to transition from a dark season to a season of dawn. Reflect on the faithfulness of God and His promise to bring new beginnings. Pray for the courage and strength to release the pain and burdens of the past, trusting that God's light will illuminate your path towards a new and hopeful season.

Day 2.   Focus your meditation on the topic of hope and restoration. Reflect on the beauty of a new day dawning and the transformative power of God's grace. Pray for His guidance and wisdom to navigate the transition from darkness to light, surrendering the past and embracing His promises of renewal and healing.

Day 3.   Meditate on the topic of surrendering fear and embracing faith during your meditation. Recognize that the transition from a dark season to a season of dawn requires stepping out in faith and trusting in God's guiding hand. Pray for the faith to let go of fear and to confidently move forward into the new season that God has prepared for you.

Day 4.   Reflect on the topic of gratitude and joy as you transition into a season of dawn. During your meditation, express gratitude to God for His faithfulness and the lessons learned during the dark season. Choose to focus on the blessings that await you in the new season, allowing gratitude and joy to fill your heart and guide your steps.

Day 5.   Visualize yourself walking towards the rising sun during your meditation. Picture the darkness fading away as the sun's rays illuminate your path. Pray for the strength to take each step with faith and hope, knowing that God is leading you into a season of greater light, purpose, and joy.

CHAPTER 3

YOUR TRUE DESIRE

*The Angel of the Lord found her by a spring of water in the
wilderness, the spring on the way to Shur. He said, "Hagar, slave
of Sarai, where have you come from and where are you going?"*
Genesis 16:7-8 Holman Christian Standard Bible

"I see you struggling, Bri. Talk to me." Cassie and Brianna sat together
after the group session. Cassie noticed that she and Rashad arrived
separately from work and didn't go home together.

Brianna patted her hair bun absently. "I don't know, Cassie. I love
Rashad. I really do, but ..." She trailed off.

"But you're not excited about him, and you know you should be?"
Cassie suggested.

Brianna nodded miserably. Her dawn wasn't filled with sunflowers and blue skies.

"Try this. When you do your meditation, first, without judgment, ask yourself what you really want. Just let the answers flow. Don't focus on Rashad. Just in general, what do you want for you?" Brianna nodded.

"Most people ruminate on all the things they're afraid of – all the things they *don't* want. Do you see?" Cassie's green eyes practically glowed with earnestness.

Brianna nodded. "I do find myself questioning my thoughts sometimes. It's like my ego speaks, then my higher self analyzes and provides a wiser response."

"Exactly", said Cassie snapping her fingers, "Not every thought you have is true. Some thoughts are planted in our minds by other people, events, or experiences. Some of your thoughts may not serve you. So think deeply about what you really want that will be best for you." Brianna nodded.

The Takeaway

Strengthening your ability to separate and discern thoughts, sensations, and emotions from your consciousness is the first step to true awareness. Harnessing this power enables you to control yourself and define the direction you really want your life to go. If God sat beside you and asked, "Where have you come from and where are you going?" how would you respond? Really think about it and assume your true desire will be granted. So, what do you really want? If you don't know, consult God for clarity and wait patiently for answers. Don't expect a big booming voice. Direction may come in the form of breadcrumbs or opportunities that lead you down a particular path. It might be a natural and gentle unfolding of your life.

Separating you from your thoughts, sensations, and emotions means you don't have to accept every thought you have as truth. This is especially important in dealing with negative thoughts about yourself and others. Brianna doesn't have to accept as truth everything she thinks about Rashad and their relationship. She can choose which thoughts to reject depending on her desired outcome.

With this in mind, think about what you really want. What do you want that transcends the bonds of materiality? What do you really want that is for your highest and best good?

My Journal Reflections

Focusing on what you want removes the focus from blaming people and situations for your circumstances. It becomes your responsibility to move towards your desires regardless of what's happening around you. Ask God to empower you to move forward. May these God-centered meditation prompts inspire you to reflect deeply on what you truly want for your life beyond materiality. Begin with a prayer and a few deep breaths. Then set your alarm for five minutes and meditate on a topic below for five minutes. Journal for greater clarity.

Day 1.   During your meditation, delve deep into your heart and reflect on what truly matters beyond material possessions. Contemplate the desires that align with God's purpose and will for your life. Pray for His guidance in discerning what brings lasting fulfillment, joy, and impact beyond the temporary pleasures of materiality.

Day 2.   Focus your meditation on the topic of cultivating a heart of generosity and service. Reflect on how you can make a meaningful difference in the lives of others and contribute to God's kingdom. Pray for the wisdom to use your resources, talents, and time to bless others and bring glory to God, shifting your focus from accumulation to selfless giving.

Day 3.   Meditate on the topic of spiritual growth and transformation. Reflect on the desires of your heart that are rooted in deepening your relationship with God, growing in faith, and becoming more Christ-like. Pray for the desire to pursue spiritual maturity, allowing God to shape and mold you into the person He intends you to be.

Day 4.   Reflect on the topic of building meaningful connections and relationships. During your meditation, contemplate the importance of investing in authentic relationships, fostering love, compassion, and support for others. Pray for the desire to cultivate genuine connections that bring mutual growth, encouragement, and shared purpose.

Day 5.   Visualize yourself living a life that reflects God's love, grace, and truth. Picture the impact you can make on others by embodying His values and principles. Pray for the passion to pursue a life that aligns with God's purposes, transcending materiality and leaving a lasting legacy of faith, love, and service.

CHAPTER 4

ADDRESS NAYSAYERS

O Parth, happy are the warriors to whom such opportunities to defend righteousness come unsought, opening for them the stairway to the celestial abodes.

Bhagavad Gita 2.32

"I want to be a lawyer," Singita blurted out. It was Sunday evening, and four pairs of eyes blinked from her computer screen in stunned silence. Then her eldest sister, Sarani, cackled, exposing the remains of the muffin she was eating.

"You? A lawyer? Why?"

"Reading eight hundred pages of *Anna Karenina* doesn't make you smart," Salma chimed in, completing Sarani's thought.

Singita's bright eyes dimmed, but she looked defiant. "It was 864," she mumbled. Then with a burst of passion she told her sisters about Barry, the lawyer in her support group whose work seemed so fulfilling.

Bhakti couldn't contain her surprise. She exclaimed, "Barry? That weird bloke with the cowboy get up and furry boots? I thought we hated him. You said he's arrogant, and –"

"I know what I said," Singita cut her off. "But he's also brilliant and kind and funny and he seems like a really good lawyer, passionate about his work. It's meaningful. He serves his firm and his clients. I'd like to do that."

"How will you tell Ammä you're not a doctor?" Sarani demanded. Singita had intentionally emphasized the word physician when she told her parents she was a physician payment and practice management specialist, and they immediately told all their friends their daughter was a rich doctor. While they disapproved of the deception, the sisters kept Singita's secret.

"And law school is so expensive, Singita," said Salma in placating tones. "How will you pay for it?"

The Takeaway

As in Singita's case, sometimes the people closest to us are the ones who hurt us the most. Being a God lover does not exempt you from this pain. Even in the case of Jesus, the one who betrayed him was Judas Iscariot, a trusted member of his own inner circle. Many motivational speakers advise that if you are embarking on a bold new venture, be careful who you share your dreams with because not everyone will cheer for you, not even your family. When naysayers surface, if their feedback is true and constructive, keep it. Otherwise, bear this in mind:

- No one can define you or hurt you without your permission.
- The most important opinion you will ever have is yours.
- Leave the burden where you found it. Often when people demean and belittle, it's more about them than it is about you. Do not accept that burden and carry it for them.

My Journal Reflections

This week's topics require deep introspection. Ask God to go deep with you and reveal truths you might have failed or refused to see before. Start with a prayer then spend at least five minutes with God before each topic. Then journal your insights for greater clarity and deeper insights. May these God-centered meditation prompts inspire you to confront microaggressions and naysayers with strength, grace, and love.

Day 1.   In your meditation, courageously confront the impact of microaggressions and the negativity of naysayers in your life. Reflect on the pain and frustration they may cause, but also recognize your own worth and identity in God's eyes. Pray for the strength to confront these challenges with grace, love, and a firm sense of self grounded in God's truth.

Day 2.   Focus your meditation on the topic of finding strength in God's affirmation. Reflect on His unconditional love for you and His unchanging truth about your identity as His beloved child. Pray for His guidance and wisdom to respond to microaggressions and naysayers with confidence and grace, rooted in the knowledge of who you are in Him.

Day 3.   Meditate on the power of forgiveness and grace in the face of microaggressions and negative comments. Reflect on Jesus' example of responding to hostility with love and forgiveness. Pray for the ability to extend grace to those who may unknowingly or knowingly perpetuate microaggressions, entrusting the outcomes to God's justice.

Day 4.   Reflect on the topic of self-empowerment and the strength that comes from knowing your worth in God. During your meditation, affirm your own value and significance, knowing that no one can diminish your worth in His eyes. Pray for the courage to confront microaggressions and naysayers, responding from a place of strength and confidence rooted in God's truth.

Day 5.   Visualize yourself surrounded by God's protective love and truth during your meditation. Picture His shield of love deflecting the negativity and hurtful words of microaggressions and naysayers. Pray for His peace to guard your heart and mind, empowering you to rise above the negativity and respond with love, truth, and a firm sense of your identity in Him.

CHAPTER 5
BE ENOUGH

Know that I am like the brilliance of the sun that illuminates
the entire solar system. The radiance of the moon and the
brightness of the fire also come from Me.

Bhagavad Gita 15.12

The morning after her jarring conversation with her sisters, Singita sat on her meditation pillow and considered Sarani's ugly words. She remembered all the times during their childhood when Sarani belittled her. She remembered her father's beatings, both with his fists and his words. Only their brother, Bhavin, and youngest sister, Bhakti, were spared. Bhavin because he was a boy, and Bhakti because Appä said she was too black to touch. Singita suspected even he could see that Bhakti was also the most beautiful.

Singita closed her eyes and visualized herself as a lawyer. There she was in a bright red suit, spiked stilettos, a leopard-skin satchel across her back, and striding confidently. She saw the sights, sounds, smells, and tasted what her new professional life would be like. Her current job had a stretched-out title that made her parents think she was important, that made her feel important. But being a lawyer would provide real fulfillment.

"I am enough." If she could be a physician payment and practice management specialist, she could be a lawyer.

The Takeaway

God created you perfect, in His image. How it must pain Him to watch you struggle with feelings of inferiority! Here you lie, God's most magnificent creation, cowering in self-doubt hoping for crumbs under His table. Don't believe *anyone* who tries to tell you that you are inferior, no matter how often they repeat it and no matter how many ways they send that message. Stand up and take your rightful place at the beautiful setting He created for His beloved child.

No one has the power to define you without your permission. Express your requests with respect, humility, and the confidence of a beloved heir.

Dislodging negative thoughts and self-perceptions so that you can fully step into the dawn of your new opportunities can take a long time. Be patient with yourself. You might have to repeat Singita's week for years, but with consistent practice, it will become easier to see yourself in the new desired light.

As did Singita, examine the motivations of the people who give you feedback in addition to the quality of the feedback itself. In doing this, Singita rejected Sarani's words while accepting the validity of Salma's question and developing an action plan to address it. All the while she affirmed her own self-worth. You can do the same.

My Journal Reflections

Spend at least five minutes in silent meditation first thing each morning for at least five days this week. Stand up for yourself even if you feel as if you are alone in your stance. It's about coming into the fulness of all the gifts you were born with.

Day 1. In your five-minute meditation, embrace the truth that you are enough in God's eyes. Reflect on His unconditional love and acceptance of you as His creation. Release the need for external validation and instead find contentment and fulfillment in the knowledge that you are deeply loved and valued by Him.

Day 2. Today, focus your meditation on the topic of embracing your uniqueness. Reflect on the specific gifts, talents, and qualities that God has bestowed upon you. Pray for the courage to celebrate your individuality and recognize that you are enough just as you are, uniquely created for a purpose.

Day 3. In today's five minutes, meditate on the power of self-compassion and self-acceptance. Reflect on God's abundant grace and forgiveness and extend that same compassion to yourself.

Release the expectations of perfection and embrace the truth that you are enough, flaws and all. Pray for the ability to love yourself as God loves you, embracing your worthiness and inherent value.

Day 4. Reflect on the topic of finding your identity in God. During your meditation, contemplate the significance of being rooted in Him rather than seeking validation from the world. Pray for the strength to let go of comparison and societal standards, and instead find your identity and worth in your relationship with God, knowing that you are enough in His eyes.

Day 5. Visualize yourself embracing the truth of being enough during your meditation. Picture yourself standing tall, filled with confidence and self-acceptance. Embrace the truth that you are fearfully and wonderfully made by God, uniquely designed for His purposes. Pray for His affirmation and guidance as you navigate life with the confidence that you are enough.

CHAPTER 6
BE DETERMINED

Trust in the Lord with all your heart, and do not rely on your own understanding; think about Him in all your ways, and He will guide you on the right paths. Don't consider yourself to be wise; fear the Lord and turn away from evil.

Proverbs 3:5-7 Holman Christian Standard Bible

Rashad was determined to have a wonderful evening with his wife when he got home from work. *Okay, God. I got this!* He sent up a confident prayer. Cassie suggested that enjoying light experiences together might quell his ambivalence about the marriage. He wore the butterscotch-yellow shirt Bri loved because it brought out the glow in his skin. He visualized them talking and laughing about their day. He even meditated on how he'd react if he came home to a cold shoulder. Today he would choose to love her no matter what mood she was in. He even bought her a bouquet.

The moment he walked through the door; he felt the chill. When he saw the sullen look on Brianna's face, he came undone. Like Frosty the Snowman, Rashad's resolve melted away, and he sank back into his old familiar ugly habits of avoidance, deflection, and passive aggressiveness in a sea of stress and resentment.

Too often we give our power away to another to define our state of mind and emotion.

The Takeaway

Without being firmly rooted in God through a consistent prayer life and mature mindfulness meditation practice, most of us are like Rashad. We know the right thing to do and resolve to change our attitudes. We even prepare to do the right thing even when we know it won't be comfortable. After all, God never promised that the right path would be easy. But when faced with the first sign of resistance, we devolve into old, negative habits.

Dawn is what you make it, and not every day is smooth. You may have to work at it repeatedly to accomplish your goal. Rashad practiced many more evenings before he could stop his mental flowers from withering under the glare of his wife's negative emotions. But with his effort, a strange thing began to happen. She became increasingly pleasant to him.

Part of the benefit of sitting in stillness is recognizing that we are not our emotions. We can observe them and choose not to allow them to drive our behaviors and derail our relationships.

My Journal Reflections

This week involves asking yourself tough questions during your reflection. Ask God to hold you safe and gently reveal the truths you need to see. Don't be discouraged if your initial efforts to change are unsuccessful. Keep at it. God will never give up on you. Don't give up on yourself. God won't.

Day 1.   In your meditation, recommit your intentions to God's guidance and seek His strength. Reflect on the purpose and goals you have set for yourself, knowing that God has called you to a specific path. Pray for His wisdom, determination, and strength to stay resolute in the face of opposition, trusting in His empowering presence.

Day 2.   Focus your meditation on the topic of resilience and perseverance. Reflect on the challenges and obstacles you have faced along your journey. Pray for the strength to remain steadfast in your convictions, trusting that God will equip you to overcome any opposition that comes your way. Embrace His unwavering support and draw upon His strength.

Day 3.   Meditate on the power of God's promises during your time of reflection. Reflect on His faithfulness throughout history and in your own life. Pray for the courage and determination to cling to His promises when facing opposition, knowing that He will uphold and sustain you. Allow His promises to be a source of encouragement and inspiration.

Day 4. Reflect on the topic of surrendering your fears and doubts to God. During your meditation, acknowledge any doubts or fears that may arise in the face of opposition. Surrender them to God's loving presence, trusting in His guidance and strength. Pray for the faith and determination to push forward, knowing that He is with you every step of the way.

Day 5. Visualize yourself standing firm in the face of opposition during your meditation. Picture yourself rooted in God's truth and unwavering in your convictions. Pray for His strength to be your foundation, empowering you to stay determined and strong even in challenging circumstances. Embrace His presence as you face opposition, knowing that He will provide the courage and resolve you need.

CHAPTER 7

THINK HIGHER

Whoever conceals an offense promotes love, but whoever gossips about it separates friends.
Proverbs 17:9 Holman Christian Standard Bible

"How did you set aside your issues and move forward in your marriage?" Singita's dark eyes burned with curiosity.

"Well, the issues are still there, but I elevated my thinking," said Brianna. "When I looked at the bigger picture, I realized how petty many of my issues were with Rashad and our marriage." Singita looked skeptical. "Don't get me wrong! I had legitimate issues. But not enough to ditch twenty-three years of marriage. And I still love Rashad."

"So, you just decided to forgive him and be happy and that was that?" Singita looked incredulous.

Brianna laughed. She explained that it wasn't that simple. She had prayed – *a lot!* "Rather than a burden, God showed me that my marriage is a gift. You view a thing very differently when you think of it that way, rather than as a problem to be endured. I started looking for the goodness and it was as if God was right there, reminding me of all I once loved and forgot about Rashad and our relationship." She and Rashad were attending marriage counseling because she had decided to do everything necessary to make it work.

The Divine: "Well done thou good and faithful servant."
The Human Soul: "Alas! If I had known this was the game,
I would have played with a much better attitude!"

The Takeaway

Brianna's issues with her marriage seemed huge until she put them in a broader context. Your consciousness is greater than the small—in the context of the vast universe—physical temple in which it resides. When you close your eyes for today's meditation, lift yourself out of your body and expand your consciousness. Visualize yourself soaring skyward. Soar into the atmosphere beyond the earth and mentally look down. How big is all that stuff now? Imagine yourself hovering above time. Imagine that you are standing above the span of your life. How important are the day-to-day ups and downs? Will you remember them a year, ten years, fifty years from now?

In your expansive state, where life is the equivalent of a single day when compared to the vastness of eternity, what really matters? How will you wish you had lived this day?

My Journal Reflections

Spend at least five minutes in silent meditation first thing each morning for at least five days this week. Remember that many of the solutions to your life's biggest problems begin with a single decision. Transcend petty issues and think higher thoughts. May God's presence and wisdom guide you in shifting your focus from the trivial to the eternal. Seek the freedom and joy that come from embracing thoughts that honor God and inspire positive change in your life and the lives of others.

Day 1.   In your meditation, seek to transcend petty issues and elevate your thoughts to higher realms. Reflect on the vastness of God's creation and the depth of His wisdom. Pray for the ability to rise above the trivial concerns and focus on thoughts that honor God, bring peace, and inspire positive change in yourself and others.

Day 2.   Focus your meditation on the topic of gratitude and appreciation. Reflect on the blessings and goodness that surround you. Pray for the grace to shift your perspective from petty issues to an attitude of gratitude, recognizing the abundant gifts God has bestowed upon you. Allow thankfulness to uplift your thoughts and bring a renewed sense of joy and contentment.

Day 3.   Meditate on the power of love and compassion. Reflect on the teachings of Jesus and His commandment to love one another. Pray for the heart to extend grace, forgiveness, and understanding to those around you. As you embrace love and compassion, you will naturally transcend petty issues and cultivate a mindset focused on higher thoughts.

Day 4. Reflect on the topic of seeking wisdom and discernment during your meditation. Contemplate the importance of seeking God's guidance and understanding in all matters. Pray for the wisdom to discern what truly matters and to focus on thoughts that align with God's truth and purpose. Surrender petty concerns to His loving care and allow His wisdom to guide your thoughts and actions.

Day 5. Visualize yourself rising above the noise and distractions of petty issues during your meditation. Picture yourself soaring on eagle's wings, gaining a higher perspective and seeing things through God's eyes. Pray for the strength to let go of petty concerns and embrace thoughts that reflect His truth, grace, and love.

CHAPTER 8
TAME FINANCES

*But remember that the Lord your God gives you the power
to gain wealth, in order to confirm His covenant He swore
to your fathers, as it is today.*
   Deuteronomy 8:18 Holman Christian Standard Bible

As he settled himself in his meditation chair in a corner of his plush basement,
Barry felt the divine presence descend on him like a warm, tingly blanket of
love and peace. The four-bedroom house was too big for one. But his father-
in-law, Mr. Gupta, had insisted on a home fit for his daughter and grandsons,
so he helped Barry with the down payment. Just as Barry's career caught up
to his father-in-law's expectations, Mr. Gupta yanked the rug out from under
Barry's marriage and persuaded his daughter to return to her father's home.

Barry accepted that it might take years to recover fully from his divorce, but his new life was recovering nicely. His finances remained his biggest concern. Better financial habits and a higher-paying job would alleviate the strain. As a new partner at the firm, the pay wasn't yet as good as the title. But what he knew for sure was that the God who had brought him this far, would show him the way. He only needed to trust, be grateful, and do his small part to bring about the financial stability he yearned for.

Five Things

Notice that Barry's situation hasn't changed since the Dark season. He still lost the love of his life and his finances are still a mess. But what *has* changed is his mindset. You can't always change your circumstances, but you can always change your perspective. And if finances are an issue, you can tame finances, no matter your life stage, with these five steps.

1. Identify essential expenses. What's left—your discretionary income—is what you'll use to start your plan for financial freedom.
2. Set aside $1,000 for your emergency fund.
3. Pay off all your debt. Start with the smallest bill and roll that amount over to the next one (debt snowball). Starting with the smallest debt will be rewarding and encouraging when you pay it off.
4. Save three to six months of monthly expenses for your fully funded emergency stash.
5. Out of every paycheck, pay yourself first, and give back by saving at least 10 percent and donating 10 percent.

Automate your plan. Have your paycheck deposited directly into your bank account. Set up automatic payments for everything you can. Automatically transfer 10 percent to your savings and donation accounts. This will increase the chances of sticking to your financial plan and freeing up your time.

My Journal Reflections

Spend at least five minutes in silent meditation and intentionally surrender to God any financial worries. Every winter some trees are stripped of all their leaves but grow full and blossom each spring. Restoration can be yours too. Be inspired to take decisive steps to tame your finances. Experience the peace, contentment, and freedom that come from aligning your financial decisions with God's principles and purposes.

Day 1.   In your meditation, reflect on the importance of stewardship and God's provision in your financial journey. Acknowledge any areas of your finances that may feel out of control or overwhelming. Pray for the wisdom, discipline, and courage to take decisive steps to manage your finances in alignment with God's principles.

Day 2.   Focus your meditation on the topic of contentment and gratitude. Reflect on the blessings and resources God has entrusted to you. Pray for the ability to be content with what you have while being wise in your financial decisions. Ask God to help you make intentional choices that align with His will and bring financial peace.

Day 3.   Meditate on the power of budgeting and wise financial planning. Reflect on the importance of being a good steward of the resources God has given you. Pray for the discipline and discernment to create and follow a budget that reflects your values and priorities. Seek God's guidance in making decisions that align with His purposes for your finances.

Day 4.   Reflect on the topic of generosity and giving during your meditation. Contemplate the joy and impact of sharing your resources with others. Pray for the willingness to prioritize giving and to allocate your finances in a way that supports God's work and blesses those in need. Ask God to help you find creative ways to be generous and make a difference in the lives of others.

Day 5.   Visualize yourself taking decisive steps towards financial freedom and stability during your meditation. Picture yourself embracing healthy financial habits, being disciplined in your spending, and making wise choices. Pray for God's guidance and provision as you take these steps, trusting that He will lead you towards financial well-being.

CHAPTER 9

CHOOSE JOY: PART 1

"May you be content knowing you are a child of God. Let this presence settle into your bones, and allow your soul the freedom to sing, dance, praise and love. It is there for each and every one of us."

St. Teresa of Avila

"Share a time that brought you joy," Cassie said. Twelve voices erupted.

"I got a *Gray's Anatomy* science book," Singita chirped immediately.

"Took my sons to a baseball game," Barry said, beaming.

"I came to the States from England," said Fiona Darby.

"Our wedding," said Gene and Jillian Adams in unison.

"I realized that Mwari loves me," mused Nandi Chaya, deep in thought.

"Who is Muah-ree? That your boyfriend or something?" Asked Barry pronouncing the word as he had heard it.

Nandi couldn't hold back the eruption of laughter that filled the room. Barry's neck turned red. "No!" She gasped. "I'm sorry to laugh but you really caught me off guard." She explained to the curious class that she was from Zimbabwe, her native tongue was Shona, and the Shona name for God was Mwari, pronounced just as Barry had said it.

Each member of the group recounted a joyous event. Then Cassie asked, "How did that make you feel?" The group agreed their joy increased. But then they went back to feeling the way they always felt because the giddiness wasn't permanent.

"Now think of a time when something really bad happened in your life." The answers flew out. Expulsion, a lost job, death of a loved one, a bad diagnosis. "How did that make you feel?" Cassie asked. "Your joy tanked, right? Then what happened? You went back to feeling the way you always felt because that depression—even if it lasted for years or returned periodically—wasn't permanent."

Prolonged joy can be attained by going within.

Barry shook his head as if trying to dislodge cobwebs. "But what about those people who seem to be annoyingly happy all the time, even when you know they're goin' through trials?" Barry cast a sidelong glance at Singita. She bared her teeth. Barry scowled and looked away.

Brianna missed the exchange. She chimed in, "I know, right? Like that friend who keeps posting about her happy family even though you know her middle child is the product of an adulterous relationship her husband had with another woman."

"Or that buddy who goes on to anyone who will listen about how much he adores his wife even though she just left him," Nandi said. Barry turned sharply, his freckled face reddening.

"How do they do it? Are they faking it?" Singita wanted to know.

My Journal Reflections

You don't need to fake your joy. Plug into the celestial fount of ever-new joy and cultivate it daily. When done with deep concentration and consistency, spending at least five minutes with God in silent meditation first thing each morning can be like recharging your internal battery of joy. When you are fully charged, you experience that joy from within and it can withstand any external circumstance.

Day 1.   In your meditation, dig deep within your soul to uncover the wellspring of joy that comes from knowing God's love. Reflect on His faithfulness and goodness in your life. Pray for the ability to choose joy despite the circumstances, finding solace and contentment in His presence.

Day 2.   Focus your meditation on the topic of gratitude and joy. Reflect on the blessings and grace that surround you, both big and small. Pray for the grace to shift your perspective to one of gratitude, allowing joy to rise within your heart. Embrace the truth that joy is a choice and can be found in every moment, regardless of the challenges you face.

Day 3.   Meditate on the power of praise and worship. Reflect on the joy that comes from lifting your voice to God in adoration and surrender. Pray for the willingness to praise Him in all circumstances, even during times of difficulty. Allow the act of worship to ignite a deep sense of joy within your spirit.

Day 4.   Reflect on the topic of surrender and trust during your meditation. Contemplate the freedom and peace that come from releasing control and placing your trust in God's loving hands. Pray for the courage to surrender your worries and anxieties, choosing joy in the midst of uncertainty. Allow trust to replace fear and joy to fill the spaces once occupied by worry.

Day 5.   Visualize yourself choosing joy in every aspect of your life during your meditation. Picture joy radiating from within you, impacting your relationships, work, and daily interactions. Pray for the strength to choose joy intentionally, even when faced with challenges or setbacks. Embrace the transformative power of joy, knowing that it is a reflection of God's presence within you.

CHAPTER 10

CHOOSE JOY: PART 2

The Lord is my strength and my shield; my heart trusts in Him, and I am helped. Therefore my heart rejoices, and I praise Him with my song.

Psalm 28:7, Holman Christian Standard Bible

"Maybe some people are faking it, but others have likely discovered a secret about joy," Cassie said, crossing her legs and intertwining her ankles like the rod of Aesculapius, "It's not defined by what's happening out there but by what's going on between your ears." Skepticism colored many of her students. "Studies show that meditation reduces stress, increases the sense of well-being, improves relationships, increases creativity, improves cardiovascular health, enhances the immune system, and can increase your ambient level of joy from within."

Some of the confusion seemed to be clearing. Cassie pushed up her glasses with her middle finger. Barry guffawed. Ignoring him, she pressed on. "Our internal joy is like a thermostat. When something good happens to us, our joy temperature increases but later goes back to its set level. Likewise, when something bad happens, our joy temperature plummets, and we fall into unhappiness or depression. But ultimately, we again return to our set level of joy. It's why you can have a brand-new car, new child, new job, new spouse, and still go back to feeling unhappy or lonely or bored."

"I think I get it," Singita said, her ponytail bobbing vigorously as she nodded. "Sometimes we assume our unhappiness is because something changed in the nature of the spouse, job, or child. But the most likely explanation is that the primary change occurred in us."

The Takeaway

Despite external events, you can achieve and maintain joy no matter what life brings.

Stop looking for joy in external things. They don't provide lasting satisfaction. Reach within and tap into God's ever-present, ever-new wellspring of joy.

If you focus on the good, the clean, the positive, you will steadily see an increase in those things in your life. Over time, and with persistent mindful practice, you can increase your set level of joy by going within and tapping into your relationship with God. Open yourself to His bottomless joy reservoir and you will never run dry.

My Journal Reflections

With deep concentration and intention, plug into the celestial fount of ever-new joy and cultivate it daily. Steep yourself in opportunities for reflection, growth, and connection with God. Cultivate internal peace and joy during your meditation, then practice holding onto it for longer periods throughout the day by being fully present in every moment.

Day 1. In your meditation, reflect on the power of forgiveness and the freedom it brings. Contemplate any grudges or resentments you may be holding onto and the weight they impose on your spirit. Pray for the strength and grace to release these burdens, choosing forgiveness and embracing the liberation it brings.

Day 2. Focus your five-minute meditation on the topic of self-care and nourishing your mind, body, and spirit. Reflect on the importance of taking intentional time to replenish yourself and prioritize self-care in your daily life. Pray for God's guidance in finding balance and making choices that honor your well-being, enabling you to serve others from a place of strength and wholeness.

Day 3. For the next five minutes, meditate on the topic of divine guidance and surrendering your plans to God's will. Reflect on the areas of your life where you may be striving or grasping for control. Pray for the humility to surrender your desires and ambitions to God, trusting in His perfect plan and timing. Allow His guidance to lead you on the path that aligns with His purposes for your life.

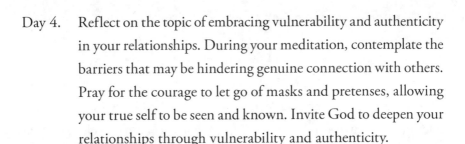

Day 4.   Reflect on the topic of embracing vulnerability and authenticity in your relationships. During your meditation, contemplate the barriers that may be hindering genuine connection with others. Pray for the courage to let go of masks and pretenses, allowing your true self to be seen and known. Invite God to deepen your relationships through vulnerability and authenticity.

Day 5.   Visualize yourself in a serene natural setting during your meditation. Picture the beauty and tranquility of God's creation surrounding you. Pray for a deep sense of awe and gratitude for the wonders of nature and the Creator behind it all. Allow this visualization to bring you peace, perspective, and a renewed sense of connection to God and His creation.

CHAPTER 11

NEVER CRY IN COURT

Though the fig tree does not bud and there is no fruit on the vines, though the olive crop fails and the fields produce no food, though there are no sheep in the pen and no cattle in the stalls, yet I will triumph in Yahweh; I will rejoice in the God of my salvation!

Habakkuk 3:17-18 Holman Christian Standard Bible

"He was so mad! He yelled at me the minute the jury left the courtroom," Heather sobbed to her boss, Barry, later. Barry was a partner at a prestigious law firm, and this was his associate, Heather's, first jury trial. As she sat curled in a mousy ball in the large chair in his expansive office, Barry could see that even with his awesome tutelage, she felt outgunned today. Her witness was unavailable for health reasons, and Heather blurted this out in open court in front of the jury rather than seeking a sidebar between the judge and the lawyers. The judge assumed manipulative intent.

Barry listened to her tale of embarrassment at being castigated by the judge in front of opposing counsel. When Heather finished, Barry asked, "Did you cry in court?" Heather shook her head.

Barry leaned forward, resting his elbows on his desk, "So what did you do?"

Heather blew her nose. "I stood there and took it. The judge was so disgusted he adjourned for the day, and I left without a word."

Barry leaned precariously back in his chair. Lacing his fingers behind his head, he grinned. "Well done!" he bellowed, making Heather jump. Clearly this was not the reaction she expected.

The Takeaway

Most professionals have had Heather's experience, a gaffe is called out in the most public and shameful way possible. You want to disintegrate on the spot.

Failure is an occurrence, not a person. Leave yesterday's event where it belongs—in yesterday.

If you are still reliving your mistake from the past, let it go today (and as many times as you need to). You cannot change it. You can only learn from it. But most important, do everything you can not to give it the power to ruin any other day in your career.

My Journal Reflections

Start with a prayer then spend at least five minutes with God in silent meditation each day for at least five days this week. Be inspired to view failure as an opportunity for growth and success. Focus on clearing your mental decks of negative past experiences and moving forward, free. Don't give your past a single moment more of power over your present or your future. If you did something bad, seek God's forgiveness, make it right with anyone you may have wronged, and *let it go*.

Day 1. In today's meditation, embrace the responsibility and wisdom that comes with facing difficult situations. Reflect on the challenges you face and the importance of approaching them with maturity and grace. Pray for God's guidance and strength to navigate difficult situations, trusting in His wisdom and provision.

Day 2. Focus your meditation on the topic of resilience and perseverance. Reflect on the trials and hardships you encounter and the importance of facing them head-on. Pray for the resilience to endure and the courage to make wise decisions, knowing that God is with you every step of the way.

Day 3.   Meditate on the power of self-reflection and self-control. Reflect on how your thoughts, words, and actions impact difficult situations. Pray for the wisdom to pause, evaluate, and respond in a way that brings peace and resolution. Ask God to help you exercise self-control and choose your words and actions carefully.

Day 4.   Reflect on the topic of seeking guidance from God during your meditation. Contemplate the importance of seeking His wisdom and discernment when dealing with difficult situations. Pray for the humility to submit your plans and desires to His will, trusting that He will provide the guidance and insight you need.

Day 5.   Visualize yourself handling difficult situations with grace and wisdom during your meditation. Picture yourself standing strong and confident, guided by God's light and wisdom. Pray for His strength to respond effectively, with love and compassion, in challenging circumstances. Trust in His presence and seek His guidance as you navigate the complexities of adult life.

CHAPTER 12

USE FAILURE

Then Job stood up, tore his robe, and shaved his head. He fell to the ground and worshiped, saying: Naked I came from my mother's womb, and naked I will leave this life. The LORD gives, and the LORD takes away. Praise the name of Yahweh. Throughout all this Job did not sin or blame God for anything.

Job 1: 20-22 Holman Christian Standard Bible

Singita aced her first practice Law School Admission Test, just as she expected. But as she regarded her score, she couldn't help asking God why she was such a failure at the relationship with Appä and why her mother always took his side over hers, even when she knew he was wrong.

Across town, Barry pondered his failed marriage and tried to shake the self-blame. He had done everything he could think of to delight his wife—weekly flowers, dinners out. He even massaged her feet when she came home from work. He was devastated when she told him she needed her parents and vast extended family she grew up with, and wanted a divorce.

The Takeaway

Sometimes you do everything correctly and still get the wrong result. In those situations, it's easy to become discouraged. You start thinking you're not good enough. You might even believe that the kind of success or happiness you seek is not meant for you. Is there any point in trying?

> *Sometimes life is a little bit crooked and sometimes it's a lot crooked. Resilience will help you recover. Optimism will help you move forward in hope. God can refuel and reenergize both those things if you lean on Him.*

When people fail at something, too often they define themselves with that event: I failed at this thing, therefore, I am a failure. Or I received a failing grade, therefore, I am not bright. Not only is this false, but it is also debilitating and marks the beginning of your internal negative voice's efforts to derail your motivation, morale, and future prospects.

Understand that life events that appear to be failures are often nothing more than course corrections. Country singer Garth Brooks once talked about the blessing of unanswered prayers because when you're older and wiser, you may find yourself deeply grateful for all the things you desperately wanted but did not receive. Today accept the wisdom and learning of failed attempts.

My Journal Reflections

Start with a prayer then spend at least five minutes with God in silent meditation each day this week. Bring before Him all the negative messages that have plagued you and seek His help in identifying their source and dislodging negative labels you or others have pasted onto your soul. Rise from the ashes of failure, embracing resilience, perseverance, and faith as you pursue your goals. Find strength, wisdom, and ultimately, success through God's grace and transformative power.

Day 1. In your meditation, embrace the transformative power of failure as an opportunity for growth and renewal. Reflect on moments of setback and disappointment, knowing that they can serve as steppingstones toward greater success. Pray for God's guidance and strength to rise from the ashes of failure, learning from your experiences and embracing the resilience to succeed.

Day 2. Focus your meditation on the topic of perseverance and faith. Reflect on the stories of individuals in the Bible who faced failures and setbacks but ultimately found redemption and success through God's grace. Pray for the faith to persevere in the face of failure, trusting that God can turn your trials into triumphs according to His perfect plan.

Day 3.   Meditate on the importance of self-compassion and forgiveness during your reflection. Reflect on the tendency to be harsh and critical of yourself when faced with failure. Pray for the ability to extend grace to yourself, releasing any self-blame or negative self-talk. Embrace God's unconditional love and forgiveness, allowing it to uplift and motivate you to rise from failure with renewed determination.

Day 4.   Reflect on the topic of resilience and learning from failure. During your meditation, contemplate the lessons and insights that can be gleaned from moments of defeat. Pray for the humility to acknowledge areas where growth is needed and the resilience to persevere and keep moving forward. Trust in God's transformative power to turn your failures into steppingstones toward success.

Day 5.   Visualize yourself rising from the ashes like a phoenix during your meditation. Picture the flames of failure being extinguished, and your spirit soaring higher than ever before. Pray for the strength and courage to embrace failure as a catalyst for growth, allowing it to ignite a fire within you to pursue success with renewed passion and determination..

CHAPTER 13
STAY FOCUSED

Let nothing perturb you, nothing frighten you. All things pass. God does not change. Patience achieves everything.

St. Teresa of Avila

Brianna was excited. The next day she would give a keynote address for her favorite foundation in front of a thousand people. But she had problems. After a delayed flight from Minneapolis and snarled Chicago traffic, she finally reached the hotel to practice her speech. But setup was in full force in the ballroom where the gala would be held. Workers milled everywhere, rolling banquet tables into place, unfurling table linens, and laying electrical cables that snaked all over the floor.

Brianna's trip to the stage was blocked by a man rolling a table into position. Crew members nearly clobbered her with a projector. She had to wait for a man laying cable to secure it to the floor. The relentless activity thwarted her efforts to reach the stage.

Five Things

You may experience Brianna's day in various ways. Calls, family members, and pets interrupt your workday. A virus cuts into your travel plans and workout routine. Or spiritually, you want to achieve daily peace and joy, but anxiety, depression, and negative thoughts keep clobbering you over the head and making it difficult to see a clear path.

God is the unwavering True North. Focus on Him allows you to hold on to (or return to) your original intention. Allow no distraction to divert your personal, professional, and other goals. If nothing else, keep your spiritual eye focused on the one who will never leave or forsake you and just trust in that relationship. He will see you through all things.

Also, you can try these five steps:

1. Get enough sleep. You may need to fight daily to maintain this discipline.
2. Create a consistent daily schedule.
3. Identify your biggest daily distractions.
4. Insert hurdles between you and your distractions. For example, work in a room with no TV, delete social media accounts, or designate after-hours time slots to catch up.
5. Reward yourself for accomplishing each intended task. Take a walk or mindful break, put that load of laundry in. Time yourself so you stay on track.

As for Brianna, despite stubbed toes and irritated workers, she finally reached the podium and practiced her speech to a group of disinterested workers. Her efforts yielded a standing ovation the next day.

My Journal Reflections

Start with a prayer then spend at least five minutes with God in silent meditation for at least five days this week. Stay focused on your goals despite obstacles and distractions. Seek His will and pursue your purpose. Like most worthwhile habits, focus doesn't just happen; it must be cultivated and given space to grow.

Day 1.   In today's five-minute meditation, reflect on the importance of staying focused on your goals, both short and long term. Acknowledge the obstacles and distractions that may arise along the way. Pray for the clarity of mind, determination, and resilience to overcome these challenges and keep your eyes fixed on the path God has set before you.

Day 2.   Focus your five-minute meditation on the topic of surrendering control and trusting in God's guidance. Reflect on the limitations of your own understanding and the uncertainties that may arise. Pray for the faith to surrender your plans to God, seeking His wisdom and direction in navigating obstacles and distractions. Trust in His perfect timing and provision.

Day 3.   Today, spend your five minutes meditating on the power of perseverance and patience. Reflect on the importance of staying committed to your goals, even when faced with setbacks or slow progress. Pray for the strength to persevere through

difficulties and the patience to trust in God's timing. Allow His grace to sustain you and give you the endurance to keep moving forward.

Day 4. Spend the next five minutes reflecting on the topic of accountability and seeking support during your meditation. Contemplate the value of surrounding yourself with a supportive community that encourages and challenges you to stay focused on your goals. Pray for discernment in choosing the right people to journey with you and for the humility to seek guidance and wisdom from those who can offer valuable insights.

Day 5. Take five quiet minutes to visualize yourself successfully achieving your short- and long-term goals during your meditation. Picture the joy, fulfillment, and impact that comes from staying focused despite obstacles and distractions. Pray for God's strength and guidance to navigate challenges and stay on course. Embrace His promises and trust that He will equip you to accomplish what He has placed in your heart.

CHAPTER 14
YOU CAN DO THIS

The LORD *helps all who fall; He raises up all who are oppressed.*

Psalm 145:14 Holman Christian Standard Bible

"I don't know how long I can do this, Singi. I feel like I'm failing at everything. The kids don't behave, the house is always a mess, Jopi is always gone, and my best friend is a parrot, literally."

Singita basked in the sun on her patio. Sameena was her closest sibling. While she felt her despair, Singita wasn't discouraged by it. She adjusted her giant multicolored floppy hat to better shield her smooth, honey-toned face from the sun.

"Your best friend isn't a parrot. It's your sister. The kids are wonderful, and your idea of a messy house is a cushion that's not propped the right way," she said.

Sameena tried to smile. Singita told her about her journey through her dark season, the peace she finally made with their appä, and how mindfulness brought her through. She even confided about her law school application. "You are not alone, Sameena. You can do this."

The Takeaway

No matter where you are in life, your self-perception is often different from how others see you. Sameena is successfully raising two wonderful children and holding down the fort. But all she sees is failure. No matter where you are, strive to move forward, but be kind to yourself.

> *Self-judgment can be crippling. If this is an issue, try to see yourself through the eyes of God, the one who loves you the most.*

And like Singita, no matter what season you are in, you will be surrounded by friends and family in different seasons. Don't sprint alone. Take time to share your journey with those you trust. If you take time to replenish yourself with the tools of self-care you have found effective, you can give away your love daily and never run dry. Pay attention to those around you who need help. Sometimes the circumstances we find ourselves in are just a path to love those we find there.

My Journal Reflections

Ask God to show you what He sees in you. As you go about your day, use a simple mantra like, "I've got this," to encourage yourself in your endeavors. Use this week's meditation prompts for inspiration to affirm that you can do anything you put your mind to. Dig deep and find within you God's presence and strength. May they empower you to step into your full potential, embracing His guidance and provision along the way. May you believe in yourself and trust in His unfailing love as you pursue your dreams and impact the world for His glory.

Day 1.   In your meditation, embrace the power of God within you, empowering you to accomplish anything you set your mind to. Reflect on the potential and abilities that God has given you. Pray for the confidence, determination, and faith to step out in boldness, knowing that with God's guidance, you can overcome any challenge and achieve great things.

Day 2.   Today, focus your meditation on the topic of divine strength in times of weakness. Reflect on the times when you doubted your abilities or felt inadequate. Pray for the assurance that God's strength is made perfect in your weakness, and He will equip you for every task and endeavor. Embrace His presence as a source of unwavering support and believe that you can do all things through Christ who strengthens you.

Day 3.   Meditate on the importance of aligning your goals with God's purposes. Reflect on the desires of your heart and how they can be used for His glory. Pray for His guidance in discerning and pursuing the paths and dreams that are in alignment with

His will. Trust in His provision and ability to empower you to accomplish what He has called you to do.

Day 4.   Reflect on the topic of perseverance and resilience. During your meditation, contemplate the challenges and setbacks you may encounter along your journey. Pray for the perseverance to overcome obstacles, the resilience to bounce back from failures, and the unwavering determination to keep pushing forward. Trust in God's faithfulness and His promise to never leave you nor forsake you.

Day 5.   In today's meditation, visualize yourself stepping into your full potential during your meditation. Picture yourself confidently pursuing your goals and dreams, knowing that God is with you every step of the way. Pray for the clarity of vision, unwavering determination, and steadfast faith to pursue your aspirations with courage and boldness. Allow His presence to fuel your passion and belief in yourself.

CHAPTER 15
LIVE COURAGEOUSLY

The yogis who have conquered the mind rise above the dualities of cold and heat, joy and sorrow, and honor and dishonor. Such yogis remain peaceful and steadfast in their devotion to God.

Bhagavad Gita 6.7

Singita bounced over to her mailbox and froze. There it was. The letter from Harvard Law School. She had secretly dreamed of this letter for years. She had been accepted to other law schools, but this was *the* law school. Since the coronavirus-19 pandemic, all the law schools developed virtual curricula. She couldn't pull this off before, but now she could attend law school anywhere in the country without having to move.

Once in her apartment, her long, orange nails rattled against the counter when she picked up the envelope with trembling hands. "Okay, God. This is it," she mumbled, feeling her heart hammering to escape from her chest. It took three tries to slide one talon under the flap. "I know You already know the answer. You just need to tell me what it is." Just as she extracted the letter, her phone rang.

"Are you at home, Singi?" asked Sameena.

The Takeaway

Sometimes we talk ourselves out of opportunities because we are too afraid to even try. We persuade ourselves that our dreams are unattainable. Without judgment or regret, think about the events in your life that have been skewed by fear:

- You passed on a promotion you were qualified for, and then had to train the fool who went for it.
- You clung to a toxic relationship because being lonely was more terrifying than bad.
- You were afraid to speak the truth, and an outcome went sideways.

Non-judgment includes acceptance.

Accept that you can't change the past no matter how much time you waste looking in the rearview mirror and rewriting things in your head.

Accept that the past could only be what it was because you were who you were, knowing and feeling what you did at that time.

Accept that the only real value the past can have is to inform what you do and who you are now. There is only now.

My Journal Reflections

Start with a prayer then spend at least five minutes with God in silent meditation each day this week. Embrace a decision to live courageously and face uncertainty with faith and confidence. Lean on God's presence and guidance as your source of strength when stepping into the unknown. May you find peace, hope, and a deep sense of purpose as you trust in His unwavering love and walk with courageous faith. Move into this day boldly no matter what happened yesterday.

Day 1.　In today's meditation, embrace the call to live courageously in the face of uncertainty. Reflect on the truth that God is with you and He holds your future in His hands. Pray for the courage to step out in faith, trusting that He will guide and provide for you every step of the way. Allow His presence to instill a spirit of boldness and fearlessness within you.

Day 2.　Focus your meditation on the topic of surrender and trust. Reflect on the unknowns and uncertainties that lie ahead. Pray for the grace to surrender your fears and worries to God, placing your trust in His unfailing love and wisdom. Allow His peace to wash over you, enabling you to navigate uncertainty with confidence and assurance.

Day 3.　Meditate on the power of God's promises in the midst of uncertainty. Reflect on His faithfulness throughout history and in your own life. Pray for the strength to cling to His promises and hold onto His word, knowing that He is faithful to fulfill what He has spoken. Trust in His goodness and let His promises be an anchor of hope as you face the unknown.

Day 4. Reflect on the topic of divine guidance and direction. During your meditation, contemplate the assurance that God is leading and directing your steps, even in uncertain times. Pray for the discernment to hear His voice and the willingness to follow His leading, step by step. Trust in His guidance as you embrace the adventure of uncertainty with faith and obedience.

Day 5. Visualize yourself embracing uncertainty with courage and resilience during your meditation. Picture yourself standing firm in the midst of the unknown, held and supported by God's unwavering presence. Pray for the strength to live boldly, knowing that God is your rock and fortress. Allow His courage to flow through you as you navigate the uncertainties of life.

CHAPTER 16
INCREASE FOCUS

Commit your activities to the LORD, and your plans will be achieved.

Proverbs 16:3 Holman Christian Standard Bible

Rashad was pleased with the progress he and Bri had made during their dawn season. Each day felt lighter the more he relinquished all the negative feelings he harbored about the marriage. "Thank you," he said aloud in prayer.

But he wanted to kick things up a notch at work. Each morning during his reflection time, he wrote down the three most important things he needed to do in order of priority. He scheduled time when he'd check emails, return calls, take a lunch break, and any other interruptions to his day; they ceased to be interruptions when planned. His schedule was constantly derailed by numerous meetings, so he blocked off entire days for back-to-back meetings. Then he blocked off other days when he would not have meetings and just work.

Throughout the day he chose to focus only on the task at hand despite distractions. If someone came into his office, the moment that conversation ended, he turned back to that one thing. He developed a mantra to focus his attention:

"This one thing I do."

Five Things

The challenge for most of us is translating vision into reality. Consider using cues that will help keep you on track. For example:

1. Pick the optimum time to wake up, so you can begin each day with the right morning routine.
2. Put your *Mindful in 5* book in your meditation spot, next to your watch or something else you need to start your day.
3. Lay out your clothes if you want to work out in the morning as a visual trigger to start your day the right way.
4. Write down or calendar your tasks if you enjoy checking off lists.
5. Set your *bedtime* alarm so you start preparing for bed and sleep at the optimum time each night.

My Journal Reflections

This week strengthen your mindfulness practice by using these prompts as you go about your day. Remember that mindfulness is about being present in the moment without judgment and without being overwhelmed by what's happening around you. Still start your day with a prayer and five-minute meditation. Then be intentional about focusing on God during your five-minute meditation. Throughout each day, try to remember to hold onto that focus and invite God to participate in each thing you are doing. Focus takes practice and time. Keep it up.

Day 1.   Throughout your day, practice mindfulness by focusing on one task at a time. Be fully present in the moment, giving your undivided attention to each task as it comes. Allow yourself to immerse in the experience and embrace the sense of flow that comes with dedicated focus.

Day 2.   Embrace the power of mindfulness in your work by cultivating a sense of intentionality. Before starting a new task, take a moment to set an intention for how you want to approach and engage with it. This can help bring clarity and purpose to your actions, allowing you to work with greater efficiency and satisfaction.

Day 3.   Practice mindfulness during transitions between tasks. Take a brief pause, close your eyes if possible, and take a few deep breaths. Allow yourself to let go of the previous task and shift your attention fully to the upcoming one. This helps create a mindful bridge between activities and promotes a sense of centeredness and focus.

Day 4.   Incorporate moments of mindfulness during your workday by periodically checking in with your body and mind. Take a few moments to observe any physical sensations, thoughts, or emotions that may arise. Without judgment, simply notice and acknowledge them before gently redirecting your focus back to the present task at hand.

Day 5.   Use visual cues as reminders to practice mindfulness throughout the day. For example, you can place a small object on your desk or set a recurring reminder on your phone to pause and take a mindful breath. Use these cues as opportunities to anchor yourself in the present moment, fostering a sense of mindfulness and awareness as you continue with your work.

CHAPTER 17

PAUSE ANYWHERE

May you not forget the infinite possibilities that are born of faith. May you use those gifts that you have received and pass on the love that has been given to you.

St. Teresa of Avila

Singita clicked off her call with Sameena, who waffled but didn't want anything. She was about to return to her Harvard letter when raucous banging erupted at her front door. Letting loose a string of curses in Tamil, her native tongue, she stormed to the door.

"Surprise!" the women yelled. Singita's crimson lips fell open. Her friends, who lived all over the country, were at her door. The group parted to reveal Sameena, holding an envelope high as if it were the Olympic torch.

An hour later, Singita was sitting at Treasure Island Resort in Welch Minnesota, waiting to see her favorite artist, Janet Jackson! Sameena corralled her five friends to celebrate her upcoming birthday. Janet sang a wonderful collection of her new music and old favorites, like "What Have You Done for Me Lately?" and "Escapade." The whole audience stomped around saluting and looking ferocious during the "Rhythm Nation" ensemble.

When she sang the song "Together Again," it was heartfelt and sunny. At the end of the song, the crowd went wild. Janet did something Singita noticed with interest. She stood very still in the middle of the stage. Then she looked up to the heavens, and stretching out a hand, she pointed to the sky. She stood still for a long beat. It was clear she was taking a private moment to commune with someone even with the boisterous horde surrounding her. It was like a calm pool of undisturbed water in the broil of a hurricane. Singita nudged Sameena, and the two stood still in harmony and agreement with Janet, amid the roiling, stomping crowd.

The Takeaway

The lesson from Janet's gesture is simple: It doesn't matter what's happening around you. Amid any physical or emotional storm, you can retreat within yourself and connect in a quiet and powerful way. Mindfulness doesn't just work when conditions are optimal. It works all the time.

My Journal Reflections

This week, practice pausing anywhere for five minutes in the middle of any task to draw on God's peace, calm, and joy. Allow His presence to envelop you, filling your heart and mind with tranquility and contentment. Experience the deep sense of peace that comes from connecting with Him in the midst of your daily activities, allowing His joy to uplift and sustain you. You can be mindfully focused even in the most chaotic time in your day.

Day 1.   Throughout your day, practice the art of pausing in the midst of any task to connect with God's peace, calm, and joy. Take a moment to close your eyes, take a deep breath, and consciously shift your focus inward. Allow yourself to experience God's presence within you, anchoring yourself in His peace that surpasses all understanding.

Day 2.   Embrace the power of divine connection by inviting God's peace, calm, and joy into your work. During a task, pause for a moment and silently offer a prayer, inviting God's presence to fill your heart and mind. Allow His peace to infuse your being, calming any restlessness or anxiety, and filling you with a deep sense of joy.

Day 3.   Integrate moments of divine pause throughout your day as a reminder to draw on God's peace, calm, and joy. Set gentle reminders or use environmental cues to prompt you to pause, go within, and connect with Him. In these moments, breathe deeply, consciously surrender any worries or distractions, and invite God's presence to envelop you.

Day 4.   Reflect on the topic of surrender and trust during your pauses. As you go within, release the need for control and surrender any burdens or uncertainties to God. Trust in His loving guidance and provision, knowing that He is with you in every task and that His peace and joy can sustain you.

Day 5. Visualize yourself tapping into God's peace, calm, and joy in the midst of any task. Picture His presence surrounding you like a gentle embrace, infusing each moment with tranquility and contentment. As you pause, imagine His peace filling your heart, His calm centering your mind, and His joy bubbling up within you, bringing a renewed sense of purpose and fulfillment.

DAY

When Day Breaks, and You Are Loving Life and Living the Dream

During the day season of your life, the sun is shining, and all is well. You are putting one foot in front of the other and living your life. Happiness and even joy come easily. And some people might mistake you for one who is unfairly fortunate.

In this season it is easy to become complacent and abandon our spiritual practices. However, it is precisely during this time of abundance that drawing closer to God becomes crucial. As we bask in the warmth of His blessings, it is essential to cultivate a deeper connection with the Divine. By immersing ourselves more deeply in our spiritual practices, we prolong the season of Day and allow its radiance to permeate every aspect of our being. In this state of mindfulness, we recognize that true fulfillment lies not in the external circumstances, but in the communion with God that enriches our souls. So, let us not neglect our spiritual journey when all seems bright and joyful, but rather, let us seize this opportune time to align our hearts and minds with the divine presence, embracing the abundant blessings of the season of Day.

And here's the secret: The sunshine of your Day season can last through the Dawn and even much of Dark. In fact, with consistent mindfulness meditation, you will experience less and less of the Dark periods because things that used to plunge you into the abyss of depression and despair are now no more than speed bumps along your life's journey.

Cultivate this sense of peace and calm equilibrium and hold on to it as long as you can. Don't wait to see what the day brings to decide if it's good or bad. Decide it will be a good day at dawn and hold on to that conviction no matter what each day brings. It might not be smooth all the time, but it will be a lot less bumpy. Fly in the sun of day!

CHAPTER 1

WHY REFLECT?

You will keep the mind that is dependent on You in perfect peace, for it is trusting in You.
       Isaiah 26:3 Holman Christian Standard Bible

The twelve watched in fascination as in one fluid movement, Singita folded herself cross-legged into her chair. Not noticing the gawking, she looked balefully around to make sure Shadow The Cat was nowhere nearby.

"I don't know why we're here," Barry Miles threw up his large hands, shattering the spell.

Cassie asked, "How many of you wonder the same thing?" Almost every hand went up. Cassie adjusted her glasses. "When God brings you through your dark season it's easy to abandon Him and jump into the driver's seat when things are going well."

"Oh, I get it!" Barry slapped a broad hand on his knee, making half the class jump. "Back when I was a criminal defense lawyer, I used to say Jesus lives in jail. You know why?"

The curious class couldn't resist. A chorus went up. "Why?"

"Because all my clients went into jail, found Him there, and as soon as they got out, they forgot all about Him until the next time some of them found themselves back there!" Barry roared with laughter, missing Brianna's deep scowl. Singita tried to mimic Bri, but she couldn't control the corner of her lip, which quirked up in amusement.

Cassie's brows rose and her head bobbed up slowly. "Right. Well, as I was saying, when things are going well in life it's easy to abandon practices you adopted when it was hard. But the habits that brought you out of your dark will prolong your stay in the day. Hanging out with God now will make life that much sweeter. Do you see?"

Both Singita and Nandi Chaya leaned in curiously. Gene and Jillian Adams looked perplexed. "How do you mean?" Jillian asked.

"If we cling to God now, we are more likely to prolong our season of day and less likely to slip back into dark. Yes?" Brianna asked.

Cassie nodded. "That's right, Bri. It's like filling a reservoir. The more you fill it with thought habits of stability, intentional calm, and presence, the less space the dark days have to take root. So even if you encounter the dark season, it might be less severe, and there will be fewer triggers to shift you back into dark."

The Takeaway

It's easy to cast aside our good habits when things are going well. Once we hit that magic number on the scale, the good eating habits terminate. Once delivered from strife, God-lovers stop praying. Once the thing that had you in the dark season resolves, you skip off into the light without a second thought.

If this describes you, consider this: If your relationship with God was strong enough to help you through your dark season, how much more will it help you in the day?

> *The good habits that saw you through your Dark season can also prolong your say in Day. Cling to God like your life depends on it. It does.*

My Journal Reflections

Start with a prayer then spend at least five minutes with God in silent meditation first thing each morning for at least five days this week. If nothing else, spend time with God celebrating His goodness in seeing you into your season of Day. Begin with a prayer and a few deep breaths. Then set your alarm for five minutes and meditate on a topic below for five minutes. Journal for greater clarity.

Day 1. In your mindfulness practice, double down on your commitment to connecting with God's presence even when things are going well. Take a moment to acknowledge the blessings and joys in your life and offer gratitude to God for His goodness. Use this time to deepen your connection with Him, fostering a sense of gratitude and extending the duration of your happy season.

Day 2.   Embrace the power of mindfulness in prolonging your Day season by staying fully present in moments of joy and contentment. As you experience positive experiences, allow yourself to fully immerse in them, savoring the beauty and blessings around you. Cultivate an awareness of God's hand in your life, anchoring yourself in His love and extending the joy of the present moment.

Day 3.   Practice mindfulness as a means to cultivate a heart of gratitude and appreciation, even during seasons of happiness. Take intentional moments throughout your day to reflect on the goodness and grace you have received. Offer prayers of thanksgiving, recognizing that all good things come from God. By consciously focusing on gratitude, you can extend the joyful season and deepen your connection with Him.

Day 4.   Reflect on the importance of mindfulness in recognizing the ebbs and flows of life's seasons. During times of happiness, intentionally pause and acknowledge the impermanence of these seasons, while still fully embracing the joy they bring. Offer prayers of surrender, acknowledging that God is the giver of all good things and trusting in His faithfulness through all seasons of life.

Day 5.   Visualize yourself extending the happy season through mindfulness and connection with God's presence. Picture yourself remaining rooted in His love and grace, even during times of abundance and joy. Pray for the awareness to fully appreciate these seasons and the wisdom to use them as opportunities to deepen your relationship with Him, prolonging the joy and contentment they bring.

CHAPTER 2
SEIZE THE DAY

The Lord is my strength and my shield; My heart trusted in Him, and I am helped; Therefore my heart greatly rejoices, And with my song I will praise Him.

Psalm 28:7 New King James Version

"I don't know if this marriage will survive. We're getting along, but I don't know if we'll be together a year from now," Rashad said.

Barry asked, "What would it look like if you stop waitin' for the other shoe to drop? If you stop waitin' for the bad thing to happen?"

Rashad squinted at him, and just then, his phone pinged. He glanced at it and looked perplexed. Barry's brows rose. "My son is trying to solve

a problem I can't help with. He's a mechanical engineering major, but I only really know software," Rashad said.

"Ask Cassie," Barry suggested. "She's a mechanical engineer."

"*Mindful in 5* Cassie?" Rashad couldn't conceal his surprise. It was Barry's turn to look surprised.

"Yeah. What do you think she does for a living, counsel schmucks like us all day?" Rashad looked ashamed. He'd never thought about it. Barry smirked. "Dude, that chick is wicked smart. Refurbishes classic cars and Harleys in her spare time. That's how I met her; we were in the same bike club. I even tried to date her, but she wouldn't have me."

"Cassie?" was all Rashad could manage.

"Open your eyes, man," Barry said. "I bet you don't even know her last name."

The Takeaway

Too many people spend so much time sprinting toward the next thing or gazing in the rearview mirror that they miss what's right in front of them.

> *Yesterday is gone. Tomorrow will tend to itself. There is only now.*

Be intentional about luxuriating in what you are doing in the present moment. Psychologists call this savoring. Barry is trying to get Rashad to savor his marriage and the present, regardless of what tomorrow might bring. Rashad's full engagement now may increase the chances that his marriage will survive and even thrive tomorrow.

My Journal Reflections

Seize the day and charge bravely into your future! Embrace the guidance and empowerment that come from aligning your life with God's will. Walk with confidence and trust in His provision, knowing that He is faithful to lead you on a path of purpose and fulfillment. Spend at least five minutes in God's company reveling at your current good fortune and all His blessings. Your life starts now. So, what are you going to do?

Day 1. In your meditation, embrace the call to seize the day and charge bravely into your future with God by your side. Reflect on His promises of guidance and provision as you step into new beginnings. Pray for the courage to embrace the unknown, trusting that God has a plan and purpose for your life.

Day 2. Focus your meditation on the topic of divine empowerment. Reflect on the strength and courage that comes from aligning your life with God's will. Pray for His grace to overcome fears and obstacles that may hold you back. Embrace His power within you as you bravely charge into the future, knowing that He is with you every step of the way.

Day 3. Meditate on the importance of surrendering your plans to God and seeking His guidance. Reflect on the beauty and blessings that await as you trust in His leading. Pray for the wisdom to discern His will and the willingness to follow His path, even if it takes you outside your comfort zone. Embrace the excitement and anticipation of stepping into the future with God as your guide.

Day 4. Reflect on the topic of embracing divine opportunities and stepping out in faith. During your meditation, contemplate the doors of possibility that may open before you. Pray for the discernment to recognize God's leading and the boldness to take action. Trust in His provision and step bravely into the future, knowing that He is preparing the way.

Day 5. Visualize yourself fearlessly charging into the future, guided by God's hand and filled with His peace and joy. Picture yourself walking with confidence and purpose, fully aware of His presence and the blessings that await. Pray for the strength to seize the day and embrace the opportunities that come your way, trusting in God's plans for your life.

CHAPTER 3

EMBRACE YOUR POWER

*Of the transient there is no endurance, and of the eternal there
is no cessation. This has verily been observed and concluded by
the seers of the Truth, after studying the nature of both. That
which pervades the entire body, know it to be indestructible.
No one can cause the destruction of the imperishable soul.*

Bhagavad Gita 2.16

"I love my sisters. I do. I just wish they would be more supportive.
Especially Sarani." Singita saw empathy brimming in Cassie's green
eyes. Shadow The Cat leered at her with his one good eye from beneath
Cassie's long brown skirt.

"What's your biggest frustration with this situation?" Cassie asked.

Singita blinked her perfectly made-up smokey eyes. Had she not just said it?

Cassie folded her long, lean frame almost in two as she leaned in to Singita and explained, "God gives us unfiltered and unconditional choice. You have the unfettered gift of choice. You have no control over the family you were born into, but you have complete control over the choices you make in your life."

> *You can't control how others behave, but you control your own attitudes, behaviors, and reactions.*

The Takeaway

Cassie's point applies to all of us. In all areas of life there is a choice of at least two things. For example, if someone maligns you, you have the choice of reacting in kind or not. If you were raised in an environment where certain negative behaviors were the norm (for example, alcoholism, domestic violence), you have the choice of continuing that cycle or not.

This absolute gift of choice carries absolute responsibility. Too often people disclaim the responsibility by saying, "I had no choice." What they really mean is they so disliked the other choice they chose to simply pretend it didn't exist. It is also a way of sidestepping ownership and responsibility for the choices we make.

The absolute gift carries absolute power to control yourself. It doesn't mean the choices will be easy or popular. Some choices you make will have agreeable outcomes, while others yield unintended lifelong consequences. But the fact remains the power to choose is always in your hands.

My Journal Reflections

Embrace the power that comes from your connection with God. Recognize and surrender to His divine guidance, allowing His power to work through you. Challenge yourself to live with confidence, knowing that you have been infused with His strength, wisdom, and grace. Embrace the power that resides within you and let it shine forth for His glory. Practice owning your choices without beating yourself up even if you didn't like the consequences. This week, ask God to reveal to you the relationship between your thoughts and actions, and the things unfolding in your life.

Day 1.   In your meditation today, embrace the power that comes from a deep connection with God. Reflect on the limitless strength and wisdom that flow from His presence within you. Pray for the awareness to recognize and embrace the divine power that resides in your spirit, enabling you to live a life of purpose and impact.

Day 2.   Focus today's meditation on the topic of surrender and allowing God's power to work through you. Reflect on the limitations of relying solely on your own strength and the freedom that comes from surrendering to God's guidance. Pray for the humility to release control and trust in His power to accomplish great things through you.

Day 3.   Meditate on the importance of aligning your will with God's will. Reflect on the transformative power that comes from surrendering your desires to His divine plan. Pray for the courage to step into the fullness of your potential by aligning your thoughts, words, and actions with His purpose. Embrace the power that comes from living in harmony with God's intentions for your life.

Day 4.   Reflect on the topic of divine grace and its power to transform your weaknesses into strengths. During your meditation, contemplate how God's power is made perfect in your weaknesses. Pray for the humility to embrace your vulnerabilities and surrender them to God, allowing His power to shine through you. Trust in His ability to use your imperfections for His glory.

Day 5.   Visualize yourself radiating with God's power and light during your meditation. Picture His divine energy flowing through every fiber of your being, empowering you to impact the world around you. Pray for the wisdom to harness this power responsibly and the courage to embrace the fullness of who you were created to be. Embrace the truth that with God, you have the power to make a difference.

CHAPTER 4
STAND BRAVELY

Fear not, for I am with you; Be not dismayed, for I am your God. I will strengthen you, Yes, I will help you, I will uphold you with My righteous right hand.

Isaiah 41:10 New King James Version

On the sprawling Lake Forest, Illinois, campus, Bri hopped on the elevator. Her coveted meeting was minutes away. Gottfried Kaufman was CEO of Sunderland Medical, subsidiary of a global conglomerate on par with Google and Amazon. He was so impressed with a speech she gave at a foundation dinner that he invited her for this meeting. Brianna was the only Black person and the only woman on the elevator. The white men were dressed in dockers, white shirts, and dark blazers.

Her dark blazer covered a tasteful African-print dress and matching jewelry she had purposefully chosen. With her lithe body, long graceful neck, and bun topped with a cascading crown of natural curls, she looked regal. She had never fit in and never would, so there was no sense in hiding. She said a prayer of thanks and smiled. *All the better to be memorable, my dear*, she thought.

The Takeaway

God created only one you, an individual with unique gifts. With those gifts you will serve purposes only you can. No one will lay footsteps in your exact pattern through life, and only you will leave this world at your appointed time.

There is only one you. As social creatures, human beings tend to seek the company of others, and we tend to seek conformity.

If you ever felt different because of your appearance or something you viewed as a peculiarity, you know the discomfort of nonconformity. If you felt at home as one of the men on Bri's elevator, you know the comfort of belonging. In that case, it may sometimes be difficult to be memorable despite a veneer that might render you invisible.

Embrace yourself and your unique skills, capabilities, and talents. They are yours on purpose, and you are perfect just as you are right now. This is who you are. Rise and soar!

My Journal Reflection

Spend at least five minutes in silent meditation with God each day for at least five days this week. Be inspired to stand bravely in the face of distractions and obstacles. Find strength and courage in God's presence as you navigate through challenges. May His guidance and peace fortify you, allowing you to stay focused and resolute on your journey. Trust in His unwavering support and know that with Him, you can overcome any distraction or obstacle that comes your way.

Stepping into the power of who you are is not once and done. It is a daily decision, and when you live life intentionally, you will become conscious of the myriad times in a day when you must choose this fork in the road during that meeting, in responding to emails, in the temptation to hide behind the wisdom of others.

Day 1.   In your meditation, embrace the call to stand bravely in the face of distractions and obstacles, knowing that God is with you. Reflect on His promise to be your strength and shield. Pray for the courage to focus on Him amidst the distractions and to navigate the obstacles with unwavering faith.

Day 2.   Focus your meditation on the topic of divine protection and guidance. Reflect on the assurance that God goes before you and walks beside you, even in the midst of challenges. Pray for His guidance to discern the distractions that hinder your path and the wisdom to navigate through them. Trust in His presence to lead you forward with courage and determination.

Day 3.   Meditate on the power of resilience and perseverance. Reflect on the stories of biblical figures who faced incredible obstacles but remained steadfast in their faith. Pray for the strength to stand firm in your convictions and to press on despite the distractions and obstacles that may come your way. Embrace the courage to keep moving forward with God as your guide.

Day 4. Reflect on the topic of divine peace and serenity. During your meditation, contemplate the inner calm that comes from anchoring yourself in God's presence. Pray for His peace to guard your heart and mind, enabling you to stay focused amidst the noise and challenges. Allow His peace to fortify you, giving you the strength to face any obstacle with grace and resilience.

Day 5. Visualize yourself standing bravely in the face of distractions and obstacles during your meditation. Picture God's light surrounding you, empowering you to stay centered and focused. Pray for the strength to resist the allure of distractions and the courage to overcome obstacles with faith. Embrace the confidence that comes from knowing God is with you, empowering you to face any challenge that comes your way.

CHAPTER 5

LONELY OPPORTUNITIES

May today there be peace within. May you trust God that you are exactly where you are meant to be.

St. Teresa of Avila

It was Friday night, and Barry was going to miss Bri and Rashad's big bash the next evening. A committed extrovert, he felt lonely stepping on to the flight from Minneapolis to Chicago on an evening when so many travelers were coming the other way. He thanked God for the last-minute first-class upgrade he received. Doubtless, this was God's favor. But he figured his disarming smile and cool kicks couldn't have hurt. He wore his comfy faded jeans and white T-shirt accentuated by his favorite two-tone Texas state heritage belt. Rockport sandals showed off what he viewed as the sexy red hair on the arcs of his toes.

But he was excited. Barry had an interview for a big job as associate general counsel of Sunderland Medical, subsidiary of the largest manufacturing company in the world.

The Takeaway

Most people don't like lonely opportunities, especially when they are the only ones working when everyone else is having fun. Many extroverts consider "me time" as anything *but* sitting in separate stillness. Moreover, you rarely hear anyone talking with glee about being the only woman, the only person of color, or the only white guy in the room.

Sometimes being lonely is really being set apart for your life's purpose.

There was only one Martin Luther King Jr., one Mother Teresa, one Mahatma Gandhi, and one Abraham Lincoln. We are all created in our own significance, so we won't be like any of these individuals. Nonetheless, you hold the power in your hand to change other people's lives for better or worse in ways only you can. The choice is uniquely yours. Decide right now to never again gripe about being "the only." If you feel the pressure to represent your entire demographic, then contribute something meaningful. That way, the next time someone like you walks through the door, he or she might not be disregarded as you were or mistaken for the help.

Lean into God and ask Him to show you your purpose in this moment and how you can embrace the lonely opportunity, and make it count. In any event, since God is always with you, loneliness is the feeling you might experience when *you* can't feel His presence.

My Journal Reflections

Set yourself apart to spend at least five minutes with God in silent meditation first thing each morning for at least five days this week. Any time you feel lonely, go back to your meditation spot and invite Him to share this time with you. Ask Him to make His presence felt in all you do as you go about your day.

Day 1. In your meditation, embrace the opportunities for solitude and loneliness, knowing that God has set you apart for a special purpose. Reflect on how these moments of aloneness can be transformative and allow for deep connection with God. Pray for the wisdom to recognize the unique calling on your life and the strength to embrace the journey, even in times of solitude.

Day 2. Focus your meditation on the topic of divine purpose. Reflect on the truth that God has set you apart for His specific plan and that He equips you with everything you need to fulfill it. Pray for clarity and discernment to understand your purpose and the courage to walk in obedience, even during seasons of loneliness. Trust that God's presence and guidance will sustain you.

Day 3. Meditate on the beauty of solitude and the opportunities it presents for deep communion with God. Reflect on the stories of biblical figures who experienced seasons of aloneness and were transformed in their encounters with God. Pray for the openness to embrace these moments and the willingness to listen and learn from God's voice in the quietness. Embrace the blessings that come from being set apart for God's purposes.

Day 4.   Reflect on the topic of divine companionship in times of loneliness. During your meditation, contemplate the truth that God is always with you, even when you feel alone. Pray for the awareness of His comforting presence, knowing that He walks beside you in every season. Trust in His faithfulness and find solace in the knowledge that He is orchestrating a beautiful plan for your life.

Day 5.   Visualize yourself embracing the lonely opportunities in life with a sense of purpose and joy during your meditation. Picture yourself growing closer to God, finding strength and inspiration in His presence. Pray for the courage to embrace the unique path set before you, recognizing that God has chosen you for a special purpose. Trust in His guidance and provision as you navigate the lonely moments, knowing that He is with you every step of the way.

CHAPTER 6
EVALUATE FRIENDSHIPS

Two are better than one because they have a good reward for their efforts. For if either falls, his companion can lift him up; but pity the one who falls without another to lift him up.

Ecclesiastes 4:9-10 Holman Christian Standard Bible

"How was your meeting?" Singita asked Brianna. She loved her customary afternoon of crossword puzzles and Sudoku. She'd invite God to sit with her when she did them. Sometimes she basked in His warm glow and other times she felt nothing different, but knew He was there. Today, she gladly relinquished her alone time to walk briskly around Lake Harriet with her friend on this sunny Saturday afternoon.

Brianna gushed about Gottfried Kaufman. "When I stepped in, he clicked his heels, bowed, kissed my hand, and said, 'Greetings, your highness." Brianna laughed.

Singita frowned. "Really? I heard his employees call him a tyrant."

"Well, he knows how to charm because he was wonderful. He pledged a hefty donation to our school." The two friends chattered on, Singita cheerfully filling the silent spaces between their conversation with happy slurps of her ice-cream cone.

The Takeaway

Friendships are valuable in every setting. Psychological research demonstrates that having a best friend reduces stress. Research also shows that employees are more likely to stay with an employer if they have a best friend at work.

> *Try this definition for the next thirty days: A friend is someone who is good to you and good for you.*

This is not gospel, but a simple barometer by which to gauge genuine friendships. If someone isn't both things, it might still be a worthwhile relationship, but he or she might just not be your friend. For example, a coach or teacher might be good for you but not necessarily good or even nice to you. A friend who leads you astray may be good to you but not good for you.

You don't need to ditch people who are not true friends. However, awareness of your relationship dynamics allows you to set realistic expectations and be intentional in how you engage, and how much of yourself you give.

Accept people as they are. It's not your place to fix anyone to better suit yourself. Take care of yourself by minding your friendships.

My Journal Reflections

Spend at least five minutes with God in silent meditation for at least five days this week. Even if you decide someone isn't really your friend, evaluate the value of the relationship. It may lie in a different avenue than you previously thought. Evaluate your friendships through the lens of God's love and guidance. Seek discernment and wisdom in cultivating healthy, uplifting, and godly relationships. Trust in God's guidance as you navigate your friendships, and may they reflect His love and grace in your life.

Day 1.   In your meditation, reflect on the importance of evaluating your friendships through the lens of God's love and guidance. Consider the impact your friendships have on your spiritual journey and overall well-being. Pray for discernment and wisdom to recognize healthy and uplifting friendships that align with God's values.

Day 2.   Focus your meditation on the topic of surrounding yourself with godly influences. Reflect on the biblical wisdom that encourages walking with the wise and choosing friends who inspire and encourage your faith. Pray for guidance in evaluating your friendships, seeking God's wisdom to cultivate relationships that support your spiritual growth and align with His purposes.

Day 3.   Meditate on the qualities of true friendship as exemplified in Jesus' relationship with His disciples. Reflect on the characteristics of trust, love, support, and accountability that mark a godly friendship. Pray for the awareness to cultivate and nurture friendships that reflect the selfless love and grace of Christ.

Day 4.   Reflect on the topic of boundaries and healthy relationships during your meditation. Contemplate the importance of setting boundaries that protect your emotional, mental, and spiritual well-being. Pray for guidance in evaluating and establishing healthy boundaries in your friendships, seeking God's wisdom in cultivating relationships that honor Him and bring mutual growth.

Day 5.   Visualize yourself surrounded by a circle of godly friendships during your meditation. Picture yourself being uplifted, encouraged, and challenged by friends who share your faith and values. Pray for the grace to evaluate your friendships with honesty and love, and for the courage to let go of toxic or unhealthy relationships. Embrace the joy and blessings that come from nurturing friendships that honor God and bring positive growth.

CHAPTER 7

MINDFUL CELEBRATION

Give thanks to the Lord, for he is good; his love endures forever.
1 Chronicles 16:34 Holman Christian Standard Bible

Barry sat on a barstool at his sun-drenched kitchen island first thing in the morning. His hands still shook as he read the letter from Sunderland Medical for the hundredth time: "Dear Mr. Miles, we are delighted to offer you the role of associate general counsel." He'd start in two weeks. The benefits package and the job itself were beyond anything he had ever dreamed of. His child support payments would increase, but there would be much more cushion for the rest of the bills. And he could even afford to use his six weeks of vacation doing interesting things with his boys. His mind rejoiced, chanting, *thank you God thank you God thank you God!*

What Barry really wanted to do was have a drink and spend the next two weeks leaping for joy. But remembering Cassie's admonition that mindfulness and meditation were especially valuable when the sun shone its brightest, he bounded down to the basement, settled in his meditation chair, rested his forearms on his thighs, and closed his eyes.

He began his *Mindful in 5* meditation by centering himself with breathing exercises. "Thank you, God!" His heart burst with joy and gratitude. Then he gave thanks for all that he had endured, including the painful end to his marriage and the divorce that brought him to this point and made him all that he had become. Before he knew it, half an hour had gone by. But when he arose, he felt rejuvenated, refreshed, and ready for the day.

The Takeaway

Hopefully your life is filled with many days like this one. Good news abounds, and the sun shines brightly on your future. You can always reflect with gratitude.

No matter what season of life, there are always reasons for gratitude.

On days when all is well, take time to catalog all the things for which you are grateful.

My Journal Reflections

Spend at least five minutes in silent meditation with God first thing each morning for at least five days this week, even if you have nothing else to say but, *thank you God!* Revel in mindful celebration when things go well. Recognize and give thanks for God's blessings and victories in your life. May your celebrations be filled with gratitude, joy, and a deep sense of connection with Him. Embrace the practice of mindful celebration as a way to cultivate a heart of thankfulness and to acknowledge God's faithfulness in every aspect of your journey.

Day 1.   In your meditation, embrace the practice of mindful celebration when things go well, recognizing God's hand in your successes. Reflect on the blessings and achievements you have experienced. Pray for a heart of gratitude and joy as you revel in God's goodness and faithfulness.

Day 2.   Focus your meditation on the topic of recognizing divine blessings. Reflect on the ways God has provided, guided, and supported you in your journey. Pray for the awareness to see His fingerprints in your successes and to give Him thanks for His abundant grace and favor.

Day 3.   Meditate on the importance of cultivating a spirit of celebration and praise. Reflect on the biblical examples of joyful celebration in response to God's blessings and victories. Pray for the ability to celebrate with a humble and grateful heart, acknowledging that all good things come from God.

Day 4.   Reflect on the topic of embracing mindful presence in moments of celebration. During your meditation, contemplate the joy and fulfillment that come from fully immersing yourself in the experience. Pray for the ability to be fully present, savoring the blessings, and expressing gratitude to God for His goodness.

Day 5.   Visualize yourself reveling in mindful celebration during your meditation. Picture yourself offering praise and thanksgiving to God for His blessings and victories in your life. Pray for the ability to celebrate with authenticity and joy, knowing that every good and perfect gift comes from Him. Embrace the practice of mindful celebration as a way to deepen your connection with God and experience His abundant love and grace.

CHAPTER 8
MINDFUL FRIENDSHIPS

Christ has no body now, but yours. No hands, no feet on earth, but yours. Yours are the eyes through which Christ looks compassion into the world. Yours are the feet with which Christ walks to do good. Yours are the hands with which Christ blesses the world.

St. Teresa of Avila

"So how are you doing, Barry? What's happening here?" Rashad asked, waving his pool stick around Barry's basement before he took his shot. Rashad came over to play pool a few times a month.

A recovering alcoholic, Barry had no booze in the house, so the two men drank sodas. He ran his large hand across his buzz cut, hair bowing like red grass to a gust of wind. "Actually, I'm doin' great."

"You've come a long way, man. I remember finding you laying catatonic that day on your couch with the child support notice on the floor."

Barry nodded, "Yep, you kicked my butt." The two men burst into laughter. Rashad had felt compelled to go visit Barry for reasons he couldn't explain. When he found his friend, he dragged Barry outside with a football and tackled and hit him with it until the two men got a nice game of two-man tag going. Then some neighbors joined in, and the afternoon improved.

Rashad grinned. "And now here you are. And you even got that job at Sunderland!" The two men bumped fists. Barry had applied for the job after a recruiter reached out to him, telling him he was the perfect candidate for a role he was trying to fill.

"God's grace. I was cryin' out for His help on that couch, then there you were." Barry said, sincerely believing it. God had opened this door and solved Barry's financial troubles when he walked through it.

The Takeaway

Barry and Rashad exhibit traits of healthy mindful friendships.

1.   Consistent connection. Mindful friendships involve consistent contact. It's best if both friends make an effort to connect.
2.   Mutual recharging. Creating a safe space to recharge together can go a long way to reducing stress.
3.   Mastermind life. A mindful friend can provide helpful insights, ideas, networking contacts, and other resources professionally or personally.
4.   Fun memories. Mindful friends can lighten tough situations. And they can laugh about anything—at least in hindsight if not now.

This is not an all-inclusive checklist. Your friendships are not deficient if all these characteristics are not present. But if you take an honest look, you will likely discern whether you have healthy friendships.

My Journal Reflections

Spend at least five minutes with God in silent meditation first thing each morning for at least five days this week. Ask God to show you the truth about your friendships. It's okay if they aren't perfect since neither are you! Experience meaningful mindful friendships. Cultivate connections that bring mutual growth, support, and Christ-like love. May your friendships be sources of joy, authenticity, and deep spiritual connection. Trust in God's guidance as you nurture these relationships, and may they bring you closer to Him and enrich your journey of faith.

Day 1. In your meditation, reflect on the gift of meaningful mindful friendships and the role they play in your spiritual journey. Consider the ways in which these friendships can bring joy, support, and accountability. Pray for God's guidance in cultivating and nurturing deep, meaningful connections with others.

Day 2. Focus your meditation on the topic of mutual growth and encouragement in mindful friendships. Reflect on how these relationships can inspire you to grow spiritually, challenge you to become a better person, and uplift you in times of need. Pray for God's wisdom in fostering friendships that align with His purposes and bring mutual growth.

Day 3. Meditate on the qualities of Christ-like love in mindful friendships. Reflect on the unconditional love, grace, and forgiveness that Christ extends to us. Pray for the ability to embody these qualities in your friendships, offering love and grace to others as a reflection of God's love for you.

Day 4. Reflect on the topic of authentic connection and vulnerability in mindful friendships during your meditation. Contemplate the value of genuine, open-hearted communication and the freedom that comes from being truly known and accepted by others. Pray for the courage to be vulnerable, to listen deeply, and to foster an environment of trust and understanding in your friendships.

Day 5. Visualize yourself experiencing the beauty of mindful friendships during your meditation. Picture yourself surrounded by friends who share your faith, values, and vision. Pray for God's guidance in cultivating these meaningful connections and for the grace to be a source of support, encouragement, and love to others. Embrace the joy and fulfillment that come from deep, mindful friendships rooted in God's love.

CHAPTER 9
STRENGTHS

Elevate yourself through the power of your mind, and not degrade yourself, for the mind can be the friend and also the enemy of the self.

Bhagavad Gita 6.5

"Did you tell your sisters you got into Harvard Law School?" Brianna asked Singita. Big brown eyes rolled to the sky as Singita's cherry lips quirked at the ends. "So, they still think you're a physician blah, blah, blah?"

"Physician Payment and Practice Management Specialist." Singita rattled off the title with practiced smoothness. When she told her parents, all they heard was *physician*. They toasted to their impending wealth now that their daughter was a rich doctor. Singita allowed them

their misconceptions. When she failed to send thousands of dollars home monthly, Appä hurled insults.

"What are your five greatest strengths, Singita?" Bri interrupted her thoughts.

Singita's brows dropped into a thick line. She couldn't think of five.

The Takeaway

Identifying our strengths can be difficult. We are much quicker to see the positive qualities in others.

This week is all about building yourself up without being egotistical. Examine and embrace your five greatest strengths. Return to this reflection whenever you need to remember the value that lies within you. Remember that five-minute meditations are a jump-start, not a limitation.

Sit for as long as necessary for each strength to really sink in and for you to fully grasp and accept them as your gifts.

You are perfect as you are right now.

If you can't think of five positive things, borrow from positive comments people have made to you and about you, even if you didn't believe them. If you are still stuck, think of a time when someone said something to you like this:

- "You have such a gift of compassion."
- "Gosh, you are so good with children."
- "You're a lifesaver! We couldn't have salvaged that project without you."
- "Thank you for being my friend. I really appreciate you."

My Journal Reflections

Spend at least five minutes with God in silent meditation each day for at least five days this week. Explore your strengths with confidence. Recognize the unique gifts and abilities God has entrusted to you. Embrace and develop your strengths, knowing that they are meant to be used for His purposes and the betterment of the world. Trust in His guidance and provision as you explore your strengths, and may your journey be filled with joy, growth, and impact.

Day 1. In your meditation, embrace the exploration of your strengths with confidence, knowing that God has equipped you with unique gifts and abilities. Reflect on the ways in which your strengths can be used to serve others and bring glory to God. Pray for the courage to embrace and utilize your strengths, trusting in God's guidance and provision.

Day 2. Focus your meditation on the topic of divine empowerment. Reflect on how God's strength and grace flow through you as you embrace and develop your strengths. Pray for the confidence to step into your God-given abilities, knowing that He will provide the necessary resources and opportunities. Trust in His empowerment as you explore your strengths.

Day 3. Meditate on the importance of embracing your strengths with humility and gratitude. Reflect on the truth that your strengths are gifts from God. Pray for a heart of gratitude, acknowledging Him as the source of your abilities. Embrace your strengths with humility, recognizing that they are meant to be used for His purposes and the benefit of others.

Day 4.   Reflect on the topic of courageous self-discovery during your meditation. Contemplate the excitement and growth that come from exploring and developing your strengths. Pray for the confidence to step outside of your comfort zone, embracing new challenges and opportunities to further develop and utilize your strengths. Trust in God's guidance and provision as you embark on this journey of self-discovery.

Day 5.   Visualize yourself confidently exploring and utilizing your strengths during your meditation. Picture yourself stepping into your God-given abilities with assurance and boldness. Pray for the courage to embrace your strengths fully, trusting in God's guidance and direction. Embrace the joy and fulfillment that come from embracing and utilizing your strengths for His glory.

CHAPTER 10
CHOOSE GRATITUDE

They sang with praise and thanksgiving to the Lord: "For He is good; His faithful love to Israel endures forever." Then all the people gave a great shout of praise to the Lord because the foundation of the Lord's house had been laid.

Ezra 3:11 Holman Christian Standard Bible

"All right everyone," Cassie said, quieting the buzzing circle of twelve. "Let's talk about gratitude."

"Why is gratitude such a big deal?" Barry asked. He rocked precariously on the hind legs of his chair, burly arms crossed, legs sprawled in front, cargo shorts boasting hairy muscled legs.

Cassie picked up a partially toothless yawning Shadow The Cat. "Gratitude isn't just fluffy foolishness practiced by privileged people. According to the article you read for today, gratitude can deliver four major benefits. Who remembers?"

Happy to know where the creepy cat was, Singita chirped, "Stress and pain relief. Gratitude is associated with the same neural networks in the brain that mobilize when we feel pleasure or socialize."

"The same parts of the brain that control certain functions such as heart rate, arousal, pain, and stress reduction," Jillian Adams piped in.

"Excellent," Cassie said.

Fiona Darby added, "Gratitude can lead to health benefits over time because it uses those same neural networks that relieve stress and engage during social bonding."

"Indeed," Cassie agreed, caressing the cat's bony spine.

"Gratitude can also improve sleep, romantic relationships, reduce the likelihood of illness, increase motivation for exercise, and boost happiness," Fiona answered.

Cassie nodded. "What else? There's one more.

"I read one study where practicing gratitude rewired the brain, alleviating depression," Rashad said.

"To some degree, yes." Cassie agreed. At the end of the session, she asked them to list as many things as possible to be grateful for over the next week.

The Takeaway

Let go of the myth that only happy people are grateful for their charmed privileges. Many people are happy—joyful even—because they practice gratitude for all that life brings. Everyone in Cassie's group was struggling with something, yet sources of gratitude could be found.

My Journal Reflections

Even if all you have to say is "Thank you, God," spend at least five minutes in silent meditation with God repeating that phrase. With each repetition, reflect more deeply into its meaning and all the things for which you are grateful. Consider practicing gratitude daily by thanking God for a few things each morning that you are grateful for even before you get out of bed.

Day 1.   In your meditation, choose and embrace gratitude as a way to align your heart with God's goodness and provision. Reflect on the countless blessings in your life, both big and small. Pray for a heart of gratitude that recognizes and appreciates God's abundant grace and love.

Day 2.   Focus your meditation on the topic of gratitude as a spiritual practice. Reflect on the transformative power of gratitude in shifting your perspective and cultivating a deeper connection with God. Pray for the awareness to see His blessings in every aspect of your life and the discipline to regularly express gratitude to Him.

Day 3.   Meditate on the importance of gratitude in fostering contentment and joy. Reflect on the truth that a grateful heart leads to a fulfilled and joyful life. Pray for the ability to find gratitude even in challenging circumstances, knowing that God is working all things for your good. Embrace gratitude as a pathway to experiencing His peace and joy.

Day 4. Reflect on the topic of gratitude as an expression of trust in God's provision. During your meditation, contemplate the ways in which expressing gratitude acknowledges God's faithfulness and invites His continued blessings into your life. Pray for the humility to surrender control and trust in His perfect timing and provision. Embrace gratitude as an act of surrender and trust in His loving care.

Day 5. Visualize yourself embracing gratitude as a daily practice during your meditation. Picture yourself offering heartfelt thanks to God for His blessings, grace, and love. Pray for the discipline to cultivate a spirit of gratitude that permeates every aspect of your life. Embrace gratitude as a transformative practice that deepens your relationship with God and brings you closer to His heart.

CHAPTER 11

LOVE ANYWAY

Those who perceive with the eyes of knowledge the difference between the body and the knower of the body, and the process of release from material nature, attain the supreme destination.

Bhagavad Gita 13.35

Singita beamed at her sisters. Since their last meeting, she had meditated on loving them no matter how they behaved. She visualized herself treating them lovingly. She even visualized her eldest sister, Sarani, reaching through the video chat screen and slapping her hard across the face. In her meditative reverie, Singita's head whipsawed, ponytail flying, and the sting left a red imprint. But she composed herself, smiled at her

sister, and said, "I love you, Sarani." She repeated the phrase until she said it with genuine affection no matter what her sister said.

> *Singita's newfound confidence was not rooted in her sisters' approval, but in all the good that God saw in her.*

Every day she visualized herself behaving and speaking in a loving manner toward each of her sisters. Some were easier than others. For Sarani, she had to really pray for patience, love, and forgiveness.

After all her practice, Singita's days of concentration paid off. She didn't fly off the handle when Sarani made her usual snarky comments. She came to her youngest sister's defense when some of the others poked fun at Bhakti, and she was her usual loving self to her favorite sister, Sameena.

The Takeaway

Too often we think of love as a noun, something we stop doing when we no longer feel it toward an activity we committed to or people around us. In this example, Singita used love as a verb, something she exercised regardless of how she felt.

Acting in love toward others eliminates the excuse of how you feel. You can love your spouse even when you don't feel like it, just as you can love your kids, your relatives, and your friends regardless of how you feel about them. You can even do your job as if you love it even if you don't.

> *Hold yourself to a higher standard. Adopt love the verb.*

My Journal Reflections

Use these prompts to inspire you to love anyway, despite how others behave. Be empowered by God's love and grace to extend compassion, forgiveness, and understanding to others. Think about how your actions can reflect His selfless love, bringing healing and transformation to your relationships. Trust in His guidance and draw upon His love as you navigate challenging situations, knowing that His love empowers you to love anyway.

Day 1.   In your meditation, reflect on the power of God's love and His call for you to love anyway, regardless of how others behave. Contemplate the example of Christ, who loved unconditionally even in the face of rejection and mistreatment. Pray for the strength to embody His love, extending grace and forgiveness to others, regardless of their actions.

Day 2.   Focus your meditation on the topic of divine compassion. Reflect on how God's love transcends human behavior and extends mercy and compassion to all. Pray for the ability to see others through the lens of God's love, recognizing their inherent worth and extending kindness and understanding, even when faced with challenging behavior.

Day 3.   Meditate on the importance of forgiveness in loving anyway. Reflect on the freedom that comes from releasing resentments and choosing to forgive, just as God forgives us. Pray for the courage to let go of bitterness and to extend forgiveness to those who have hurt or wronged you. Embrace the transformative power of love and forgiveness in relationships.

Day 4.   Reflect on the topic of selfless love during your meditation. Contemplate the sacrificial love exemplified by Christ, who gave Himself for the sake of others. Pray for the willingness to lay aside personal agendas and expectations, and to love others selflessly, even when faced with challenging behavior. Embrace the call to be a vessel of God's love, shining His light in every interaction.

Day 5.   Visualize yourself embodying God's love and grace during your meditation. Picture yourself responding to challenging behavior with patience, compassion, and kindness. Pray for the strength to love anyway, knowing that God's love within you is greater than any negative behavior. Embrace the opportunity to be a conduit of His love, reflecting His character in all your relationships.

CHAPTER 12
FIND CONTENTMENT

The man who trusts in the Lord, whose confidence indeed is the Lord, is blessed. He will be like a tree planted by water: it sends its roots out toward a stream, it doesn't fear when heat comes, and its foliage remains green. It will not worry in a year of drought or cease producing fruit.
Jeremiah 17:7-8 Holman Christian Standard Bible

Rashad and Brianna sat cross-legged on their meditation pillows facing each other. Hands resting lightly on their knees, they gazed at each other and smiled. For the first time in a long while, Brianna thanked God for her husband as she admired his handsome face and caring eyes.

"Our kids are still gone," Brianna said.

"We are still adjusting," Rashad replied.

"I choose you anyway," said Brianna.

"I love you more every day," Rashad said.

They were on different pages of their *Mindful in 5* book. They read their books in silence and afterward, closed their eyes to meditate on their individual topics.

The Takeaway

Reestablishing an intimate emotional connection with a loved one begins with a choice followed by action. Likewise, falling in love with the life you have right now is a choice. The following five factors can lead to greater fulfillment.

1. Decide to love the life you have right now. Rain falls into every life. Accept that yours is exactly what it should be right now.

2. Eliminate feelings of entitlement. Thoughts like, *I should have,* and *I should be,* sow discontentment and frustration.

3. Live in the present. Yesterday is gone and can't be changed. Worrying won't change tomorrow. Enjoy the moment you have right now.

4. Do something nice for someone. Our self-focused society encourages us to always be concerned with our own comfort. Step outside yourself and experience the joy of giving.

5. Set goals and take the first step to achieving that thing you've always wanted to do. Being mindfully present does not absolve you of the need to plan and set goals for your life. Planning also helps you to feel a sense of purpose in where you are going that will hopefully resolve any need to worry about the future.

My Journal Reflections

This week, practice finding contentment in any situation. Discover the peace and fulfillment that come from trusting in God's plan and embracing His presence. May gratitude and an eternal perspective guide you towards contentment, regardless of the challenges or blessings that life presents. Trust in His faithfulness, and experience a deep and lasting contentment that surpasses all understanding.

Day 1. In your meditation, embrace the pursuit of contentment in any situation, knowing that God's presence and provision are sufficient. Reflect on the truth that true contentment comes from a deep sense of connection with Him, rather than external circumstances. Pray for the ability to find contentment in every season, resting in the assurance of His love and care.

Day 2. Focus your meditation on the topic of divine trust and surrender. Reflect on the peace and contentment that come from placing your trust in God's perfect plan. Pray for the willingness to surrender your desires and expectations, embracing His will for your life. Find contentment in the knowledge that He is working all things for your ultimate good.

Day 3. Meditate on the importance of gratitude as a pathway to contentment. Reflect on the blessings and gifts God has bestowed upon you. Pray for the awareness to cultivate a grateful heart, even in challenging circumstances. Embrace the practice of gratitude as a means to shift your focus from what is lacking to the abundance of God's goodness.

Day 4.   Reflect on the topic of eternal perspective during your meditation. Contemplate the truth that this earthly life is temporary, and true fulfillment lies in the eternal relationship with God. Pray for the ability to set your heart and mind on heavenly things, finding contentment in the knowledge that your ultimate home is with Him.

Day 5.   Visualize yourself finding contentment in any situation during your meditation. Picture yourself anchored in God's peace and presence, regardless of the external circumstances. Pray for the strength to release the need for control and to trust in His perfect timing and provision. Embrace the contentment that comes from resting in His love and sovereignty..

CHAPTER 13
CELEBRATE MILESTONES

Reflect upon the providence and wisdom of God in all created things and praise Him in them all.

St. Teresa of Avila

"Celebrate every milestone, no matter how big or small," Cassie said. Most were too busy studying her to listen. "Barry, what's your milestone?"

Barry the Cheshire exposed all fifty-seven teeth, "My divorce is done, my sons are thriving, and I got this amazing new job. God is good!"

"All the time!" shouted Brianna and Rashad simultaneously.

The group broke into applause.

"I finally did my *Mindful in 5* meditations five consecutive days," said Singita, bangles chiming and ponytail bobbing. "God is…good?" She said it with the hesitation of an unfamiliar refrain.

"All the time!" shouted the group in unison, delight shining on their faces.

"What about you, Cassie?" asked Rashad, staring at her. Murmurs of agreement followed as twelve pairs of eyes stared. Slowly she rose and pirouetted. Gone were the drab, flannel, shapeless skirts and dresses. They were replaced by a white, low-cut cami shirt and a dark blazer. A bulky necklace showed off her long, slender neck. High-rise skinny jeans accentuated her lean frame. Flesh-colored heels punctuated the ensemble, adding to her height. The pale ginger bush at the nape of her neck was replaced by a trendy, short, vibrant, curly cut complete with fresh highlights. She moved with a dancer's grace that hadn't been there before she began feeling as beautiful on the outside as she felt inside.

Rousing applause.

"You look like a tall, green-eyed Meg Ryan," Barry blurted.

"Don't you need your glasses?" Nandi Chaya asked.

"Contacts." Cassie beamed. Some wanted to know how the transformation happened. "Girls' day out with them," sang Cassie, pointing at Brianna and Singita.

The Takeaway

If you can first think it, you can do it, and then you can be it.

As with Singita, it might take a lot of mental energy and continued practice to take steps toward your goal. The journey may feel like a slog, not at all sexy or glamorous. But the path to great success is often paved with sweat, doubt, and tears. Trust God in all your ways, and He will guide your path. The outcome can look like Cassie.

My Journal Reflections

This week, take time to celebrate milestones, big and small. Recognize the significance of each step forward and honor God's faithfulness in your life. Use gratitude and mindfulness to guide your celebrations, and find joy in sharing these moments with others. Trust in God's presence and guidance as you mark milestones and embrace the opportunity to give Him praise and thanksgiving. Ask Him for guidance in your future plans.

Day 1. In your meditation, embrace the practice of celebrating milestones, big and small, as an opportunity to honor God's faithfulness and goodness. Reflect on the progress and achievements you have made along your journey. Pray for the ability to appreciate the significance of each milestone, recognizing that every step forward is a testament to God's grace and guidance.

Day 2. Focus your meditation on the topic of gratitude and celebration. Reflect on the biblical examples of joyful celebrations and feasts to commemorate God's blessings and provisions. Pray for a heart of gratitude that recognizes the importance of marking milestones as a way to express thanksgiving and praise to God for His abundant grace.

Day 3.   Meditate on the importance of reflection and mindfulness during times of celebration. Reflect on the moments of growth, breakthroughs, and answered prayers that have led you to the present milestone. Pray for the ability to be fully present in the celebration, appreciating the journey and the lessons learned along the way. Embrace the opportunity to reflect on God's hand in your life and give Him glory.

Day 4.   Reflect on the topic of community and sharing in the celebration of milestones. During your meditation, contemplate the importance of gathering with loved ones to commemorate and share in the joy of reaching significant points in your journey. Pray for the blessing of supportive relationships and the joy of celebrating together, knowing that God often works through the encouragement and presence of others.

Day 5.   Visualize yourself taking time to celebrate milestones, big and small, during your meditation. Picture yourself expressing gratitude, offering prayers of thanksgiving, and embracing the joy of the moment. Pray for the awareness to recognize and honor milestones in your life, both in a personal and communal setting. Embrace the practice of celebration as a way to acknowledge God's faithfulness and to inspire others along their own journeys.

CHAPTER 14

HOW GOD FEELS

Happiness is determined more by one's state of mind than by external events.

Dalai Lama [Tenzin Gyatso]

Cassie tossed her new curls and gazed around the room. "Here's my burning question for all of you. Have you experienced God in your lives?"

Heads nodded.

"Yeah!" Barry practically yelled. He described his lowest day, when his divorce lawyer sent him the child support calculation for his sons that buried him in terror. "I couldn't move. I couldn't do anything. I just laid on my couch thinkin' God help me. God help me."

"And did He?" Nandi Chaya asked with interest.

"Yup! He sent me Rashad to drag me off the couch and cheer me up." Barry looked at his friend in gratitude. Rashad smiled with a nod. Barry continued, "That night when I sat down to meditate, I felt the deepest peace I've ever known. It was a warm tingly feeling – like – like…" He struggled to explain.

"Like goose bumps all over but you weren't cold," Singita offered.

"Yeah!" Barry snapped his fingers at her. "That's exactly it! And it wasn't just peace for that moment. It was like – like…"

"Like the deepest love and peace that would outlast your very lifespan," Jillian chimed in.

Startled, Barry looked at her. It was as if these people had been in his meditation space with him. And wasn't this the same Jillian who had been so skeptical? Who had suffered so much in life and wondered if God existed? But now here she was, beaming at him as if they shared a secret. Her husband, Gene, sat next to her, a placid vacant smile on his face.

The Takeaway

In the moment, God didn't start by raining money down from the sky to solve Barry's financial problems. Barry experienced God's comforting hand, first through Rashad, who felt prompted to check on him. Then, because Barry had been in the habit of sitting with God daily, he was able to feel the direct love and peace of God's presence long before his situation changed.

> *Sometimes, all we need is to remember that this life is temporal. Whether you are materially wealthy or homeless on the street, as long as you can feel that God is with you, you have riches noone can ever take away.*

Journal Reflections

Spend at least five minutes reflecting with openness and gratitude on how you have felt God show up in your life. Reflect on all the ways you experience God's presence. Did you dismiss His work as coincidence? Did you think yourself unworthy of His attention, so you dismissed Him? Rethink and revisit these times without shame. Try to recognize His hand at work in both the extraordinary and ordinary moments of your life. Find solace, guidance, and joy in His constant companionship. Trust in His faithfulness and may your awareness of His presence deepen your relationship with Him, bringing you closer to His heart.

Day 1.   In your meditation, reflect on the various ways you experience God's presence in your life. Contemplate the moments of divine connection, guidance, and comfort you have encountered. Pray for the awareness to recognize and appreciate these encounters, embracing a deeper sense of gratitude and awe for God's ever-present love.

Day 2.   Focus your meditation on the topic of divine providence. Reflect on the times when God has orchestrated circumstances or answered prayers in ways that revealed His presence and care. Pray for the ability to see His hand at work in both the big and small moments of your life. Embrace the reassurance that He is always with you, guiding and providing for your needs.

Day 3.   Meditate on the importance of stillness and silence in experiencing God's presence. Reflect on the moments of peace and clarity when you feel His gentle whisper or sense His overwhelming peace. Pray for the willingness to create

intentional space for quiet reflection, allowing His presence to permeate your heart and mind. Embrace the beauty of finding solace and connection with God in moments of stillness.

Day 4.   Reflect on the topic of divine companionship in your everyday life. During your meditation, contemplate the ways in which God walks alongside you, offering comfort, wisdom, and strength. Pray for the ability to cultivate a deep awareness of His constant presence, even in the mundane or challenging moments. Embrace the reassurance that you are never alone and that He is always there to guide and support you.

Day 5.   Visualize yourself recognizing and experiencing God's presence in different aspects of your life during your meditation. Picture moments of worship, nature, relationships, or even the simple tasks of daily living where you feel a deep connection to Him. Pray for the openness to fully embrace and cherish these encounters, allowing them to deepen your relationship with God. Embrace the joy and gratitude that come from acknowledging and experiencing His presence in every aspect of your life.

CHAPTER 15

HOW GOD SPEAKS

Then He said, "Go out and stand on the mountain in the Lord's presence." At that moment, the Lord passed by. A great and mighty wind was tearing at the mountains and was shattering cliffs before the Lord, but the Lord was not in the wind. After the wind there was an earthquake, but the Lord was not in the earthquake. After the earthquake there was a fire, but the Lord was not in the fire. And after the fire there was a voice, a soft whisper. When Elijah heard it, he wrapped his face in his mantle and went out and stood at the entrance of the cave.

1 Kings 19:11-13 Holman Christian Standard Bible

Cassie listened carefully to Barry's comments smiling and nodding. She prompted the others for their experiences.

"God helped me find my keys," Gene Adams said.

"Seriously?" Barry guffawed.

"How many of you have children?" Cassie inquired. Half the twelve in the room raised their hands, Barry included.

"When your kids were little, how often did you kiss a scrape or comfort your baby when they cried over something that was minor to you but a big deal for them?" Heads nodded. "God loves you even more than you love your babies. So yes, whether you're having a personal financial crisis, at a marital crossroads, or whether you simply misplaced your keys, God cares." She went back to her question, asking if anyone else wanted to share how God had spoken.

"I refer to God as my Divine Mother. I just can't do the "father" thing after my experience with Appä. But I did experience God's presence in the way Barry was describing. He didn't speak in words, but I just felt a *knowing* that Appä has his own issues that have nothing to do with me and I shouldn't take them personally. What I *can* do is trust that my Divine Mother can give me all the love my parents couldn't. And that's more than enough." Heads nodded in appreciation in the silent pause that followed.

Rashad waved his hand in a hesitant gesture. Then he said, "This might sound crazy, but God came to me in a dream." He explained how he had been ready to overdose on pills until he received the warning in the dream that pills would only make his situation worse.

"How do you know that was God?" Fiona Darby asked.

The Takeaway

This is the big question, isn't it? How do you know when God is speaking to you and when a dream is just a dream? God speaks to us in many ways. He might occasionally be a directive voice in your head that tells you something you know couldn't have possibly come from you. But more often, He doesn't ride in like a mighty gale, fire, or an earthquake. Instead, He might speak in a soft whisper. He might download deep understanding or a different perspective about an issue you've been wrestling with. He might send someone just in time to help you or answer something you asked God. And the deliverer may have no idea that you were asking God for this help. He might open doors or create new pathways that solve your problem.

God speaks to you in the unique language your heart will understand. As you get to know Him better, your ability to watch for Him and see His hand move in your life will improve.

My Journal Reflections

Just keep building on that relationship by sitting with Him. He is always with you. Have faith that He's there, even when you don't feel anything. Even when there's nothing wrong. Even when all you have to say is, "Thank you, thank you, thank you." He is always there. Reflect on all the ways God speaks to you directly, through nature, and through others. Cultivate a receptive heart to hear His voice and discern His guidance. Trust in His faithfulness and allow His words to resonate deeply within you, guiding you along the path of His purpose and love.

Day 1.   In your meditation, reflect on the myriad ways God speaks to you directly. Contemplate the moments of divine revelation, where you have felt a deep sense of connection and received guidance, comfort, or inspiration. Pray for the openness to recognize and embrace His direct communication, knowing that He desires to speak intimately to your heart.

Day 2.   Focus your meditation on the topic of God's voice in nature. Reflect on the beauty, intricacy, and awe-inspiring elements of creation that reveal God's presence and wisdom. Pray for the ability to tune into the whispers of God in the natural world around you, finding solace, inspiration, and a deep sense of wonder in His creation.

Day 3.   Meditate on the importance of listening to God's voice through others. Reflect on the wisdom, encouragement, and insight that can be found in the words and actions of those around you. Pray for discernment to recognize the voice of God speaking through others, and for the humility to receive their messages with an open heart. Embrace the gift of community and the opportunity to learn from one another.

Day 4.   Reflect on the topic of divine confirmation in your meditation. Contemplate the ways in which God affirms His will and speaks to you directly through His Spirit, through the beauty of nature, and through the words and actions of others. Pray for the discernment to recognize these confirmations and the faith to trust in God's guidance. Embrace the comfort of knowing that He is actively communicating with you through various channels.

Day 5.   Visualize yourself attuned to God's voice, both direct and indirect, during your meditation. Picture yourself listening, receiving, and responding to His messages with a heart of obedience and surrender. Pray for the willingness to cultivate a deep awareness of God's communication in your life, drawing closer to Him and allowing His words to shape your thoughts, actions, and relationships.

CHAPTER 16
HOW TO TALK TO GOD

We don't need more money, we don't need greater success or fame, we don't need the perfect body or even the perfect mate. Right now, at this very moment, we have a mind, which is all the basic equipment we need to achieve complete happiness.

Dalai Lama [Tenzin Gyatso]

Cassie looked around the room at her twelve mindfulness students. She marveled at how far they had come in their personal journeys since the first day they strode, ambled, and bounced in. "Is there anything we haven't covered that anyone would like to share?" she asked, shrugging the day's tension from her shoulders.

Fiona Darby raised a tentative hand. Cassie nodded her encouragement and Fiona began in her clipped English accent. "Throughout this year I've been struggling with feelings of loneliness and isolation. I have always been skeptical of religion. I'm from the UK and when I was growing up, religion was a ritual that required you to go to church every Sunday. You sat in mass, genuflected, and bowed your head when you were supposed to. The priest prayed to God for you but you never had real time to talk to Him yourself. I don't remember anyone in my life ever telling me to go hang out with God just to spend time with Him. What a weird idea! Who does that? How do you build a relationship with someone you can't see, touch, and feel?"

Fiona was trembling, but when she looked around, heads were nodding in understanding. She continued, "But as I listened to the stories and experiences we shared in this class, I began to question my beliefs. I did sit down and try meditating. I didn't know what to say. But Cassie said speak to God in the language of your heart, so I just said that; God I don't know if you're there. I don't know what to say to you, but I'm here because I'm open to getting to know you."

"And what happened?" Brianna was curious.

"Well, I felt His presence. It felt like tangible love – the deepest love I've ever known. Like fathomless joy. Like my spirit is one with Him and nothing can ever touch me even if my body is maimed or harmed." A tear trickled down her cheek and she swiped at it with her sleeve. "I started reading books and I even went to a church service in search of a deeper understanding."

"And?" Cassie prompted her.

"I'm still at the beginning of my journey. I'm sure I'm not saying what I'm supposed to say to God. But I am speaking from my heart. I apologized for all the wrong I've done and invited Him into my life. I'm asking Him to show me what it is to have a relationship with someone

I can't see, touch, and feel. I'm asking Him to show me how to listen to Him and trust Him."

As the group ended their meeting, they held hands and recited a prayer together. Fiona felt a sense of unity and belonging, knowing that she was a part of something greater than herself.

The Takeaway

There isn't one way to talk to God. As you can see from the group members, simply asking for help in your darkest hour, like Barry did, can be enough. Even questioning His existence and sincerely asking for guidance like Fiona did, can be enough. The most important thing (in this writer's opinion) is to approach Him with respect and sincerity. You wouldn't respond well to someone who doesn't know you but shows up in your face with accusations, disrespect, and venom. God is not your genie there to do your bidding. Why would you expect Him to respond well to that approach?

My Journal Reflections

Even if the cry of your heart is you don't know how to do this relationship thing with God, start there and invite Him to show you. Explore the different ways to talk to God. Find joy and comfort in knowing that He welcomes all forms of communication and that there are endless possibilities to engage with Him. Talk to Him. Sing to Him. Laugh with Him. Take Him on a "date" when you go to exercise, run errands, or even to an event by yourself. Ask Him to hold you when you're sad and see what happens. Discover new and meaningful ways to express your thoughts, feelings, and desires, deepening your relationship with Him. Trust in His presence and guidance as you explore the diverse ways to talk to God, knowing that He is always ready to listen and respond with love. Then know with confidence that when your heart is sincere, He will answer you. Keep coming back to meditate on Him until He does.

Day 1.   In your meditation, explore the different ways to talk to God, knowing that He welcomes all forms of communication. Reflect on the traditional practice of prayer and its power to connect with Him. Pray for the openness to express your deepest thoughts, feelings, and desires to God, knowing that He listens with love and understanding.

Day 2.   Focus your meditation on the topic of contemplative silence. Reflect on the beauty and significance of silent moments, where you can simply be in God's presence and listen attentively to His still, small voice. Pray for the discipline to create intentional space for silence, allowing God to speak to your heart in the midst of stillness.

Day 3.   Meditate on the importance of journaling or writing as a way to talk to God. Reflect on the power of putting your thoughts, prayers, and reflections on paper, creating a sacred dialogue between you and God. Pray for the inspiration to express yourself through writing, knowing that your words are heard by the One who knows you intimately.

Day 4.   Reflect on the topic of worship and praise during your meditation. Contemplate the ways in which music, singing, or other forms of artistic expression can become a channel to communicate with God. Pray for the openness to engage in heartfelt worship, allowing your voice and creativity to become offerings of love and adoration.

Day 5.   Visualize yourself exploring different ways to talk to God during your meditation. Picture yourself engaging in conversational prayer, silent contemplation, writing, or any other form of communication that resonates with your spirit. Pray for the willingness to experiment and explore, knowing that God delights in the diverse ways His children seek to connect with Him.

CHAPTER 17
THE LAST CLASS

Trust in the Lord and do good; dwell in the land and enjoy safe pasture. Take delight in the Lord, and he will give you the desires of your heart.

Psalm 37:3-4 New International Version

"Thank you for attending this group." Cassie's intelligent eyes held their customary compassion as she beamed at the group. "What have you learned?"

Singita mumbled something about that scruffy cat. The other eleven were so busy smiling and nodding that no one spoke.

"BAM!" Cassie yelled, startling them but bringing out all of Barry Andrew Miles's fifty-seven teeth at a hundred watts.

"Well, Cassie, thanks to y'all and my *Mindful in 5* book and practice, I made peace with my divorce. I love my wife, and I hate that she left. But it's alright, and I have really bonded with my boys. In all that, I learned how to lean on God not just so He can carry me through my dark days, but I celebrate and thank Him when things are goin' right," Barry said, conjuring Shadow The Cat and stroking him vigorously. The cat vibrated from rumbles of delight even as he seemed to contemplate escape. "I thank God for this group every day, y'all. If it weren't for you, I'd probably be back at the bottom of the bottle right now." he said ruefully.

Next was Singita. "God helped me to finally forgive and let go of my issues with Appä. My earthly parents aren't perfect, but my Divine Mother is perfect and Her love is always mine to receive and accept. It took a lot of hard work, prayer, and support from my friends." Singita attempted a smile. It was beautiful, but she always looked awkward when she smiled, as if she didn't grow up doing it. But the class smiled back warmly. "Things are much better between me and my eldest sister, Sarani. She's still a condescending witch, but I accepted her as she is, so she's my condescending witch!" Everyone laughed. "Ironically, our getting along better has strengthened the bond between all my sisters, so I'm grateful."

Nandi Chaya said, "I've learned to look for evidence of God's hand and voice in my life. It might be the still small voice in my heart, or the insightful answer that comes at dawn to an issue I was grappling with the night before. Sometimes it's a conversation with another just when I need it, the kiss of the sun and breeze on my cheek, or a beautiful deer in my path that reminds me of the beauty and grace of God."

Rashad beamed tenderness at his wife and held out his palm. She clasped it tightly. He said, "I learned that God loves all His children, and He won't exact my revenge just because it suits me. Thank goodness."

Brianna added, "I learned that God is not a helicopter parent who swoops in and saves me from my bad choices or the choices of others. I have to take responsibility for my own choices and be accountable for the consequences of my actions." She laughed. "Cassie, you said start with five minutes, but there were times I swear Rashad sat for hours!"

"Grappling with the challenges of life takes time," Cassie said. When the couple invited the group to the ceremony for the renewal of their vows, cheers went up. "What about you, Jillian? Did you learn anything interesting?"

Jillian Adams gave a single sharp toss of her bob and took a deep inhale and exhale before speaking. Then she said, "When Gene dragged me to this class…" she paused to cast her husband a slitted glance. Gene paid her no mind. "I was angry at God for not helping me throughout my life. But through this group, I realized my troubles were often caused by my own decisions or others' choices. Despite my anger, I saw how God had been there for me, guiding and comforting me."

"So, what's your mindset now?" Fiona wanted to know.

Jillian pursed her lips in thought. She said, "Now, it's fair to say I'm cautious but open. I've felt His presence. I felt…um…loved. I may stumble, but I'm hopeful for healing and purpose ahead."

A chorus of supportive murmurs went up. After all had shared, the group departed with hugs and promises to get together socially.

Even after the group disbanded, they continued to support Fiona Darby and Jillian Adams in their spiritual journeys, offering guidance and encouragement along the way. They recognized the courage it took to embrace a new way of thinking and welcomed them into the God lovers' family with open arms.

Through mindfulness and the support of the group, Fiona was able to discover a deeper sense of connection to the world around her.

Through the practice of mindfulness and the acceptance of God, Fiona found a new sense of hope and purpose in her life.

Jillian left the meeting feeling grateful for the support and encouragement of the group, and she knew that she was on a path towards a more fulfilling and meaningful life. She felt a sense of peace and purpose in her life, and she knew that she was not alone in her struggles.

My Journal Reflections

This week, celebrate all you have learned about the God lovers' journey through your contemplation of the Divine. Embrace the ongoing process of learning, growing, and transforming as you deepen your understanding of God's nature and teachings. May your encounters with the Divine shape your character, guide your actions, and inspire you to extend love and compassion to others. Trust in the guidance of the Holy Spirit as you continue on this beautiful journey of seeking and experiencing the Divine.

Spend at least five minutes with God in silent meditation first thing each morning for at least five days this week. Take time to reflect on your mindfulness journey, the discipline you have harnessed, and how you have grown.

Day 1.   In your meditation, reflect on all you have learned about the God lovers' journey by immersing yourself in the contemplation of the Divine. Contemplate the insights and wisdom you have gained through your experiences, studies, and encounters with God. Pray for the humility to recognize the vastness of the Divine and the willingness to continue learning and growing in your understanding.

Day 2. Focus your meditation on the topic of divine revelation. Reflect on the ways in which God has unveiled His nature, character, and teachings to humanity throughout history. Pray for the wisdom to discern His truths and the grace to integrate them into your daily life. Embrace the journey of ongoing revelation and the deepening understanding of the Divine.

Day 3. Meditate on the importance of personal transformation through the knowledge of the Divine. Reflect on the ways in which encountering God and deepening your understanding of His nature have shaped your beliefs, values, and actions. Pray for the continued growth and refinement of your character, guided by the insights gained from your connection with the Divine.

Day 4. In your meditation, reflect on how you will continue your practice of connecting with God through meditation. Contemplate the importance of consistency and discipline in nurturing your spiritual journey. Pray for the commitment to set aside regular time for meditation, allowing it to deepen your relationship with God and bring you closer to His heart.

Day 5. Visualize yourself sharing the practice of meditation with someone who could benefit from learning how to meditate. Reflect on the impact that introducing this transformative practice could have on their spiritual growth and well-being. Pray for the opportunity to share *Mindful in 5* and your knowledge and experiences with others, guiding them in developing their own meditation practice as a means to connect with God and experience inner peace.

EPILOGUE

Akar, VP of sales at Sunderland Medical, raised his glass. Chantelle, the company's chief legal officer, had invited him to meet her friends, Rashad and Brianna, at a party she threw after they renewed their vows. "To weathering work!" Akar cried with aplomb.

"To weathering work," Chantelle, repeated. They clinked glasses. "Thank you for being so patient with me, Chantelle. My mindfulness meditation practice made all the difference." Chantelle bowed her head, smiling. She sipped while Akar chugged, burped, and wiped his mouth with the back of his hand.

He looked around. "Where is everybody?" he asked. Chantelle's home was a well-orchestrated open floor plan perfect for fluid movement. But the guests had disappeared.

Chantelle nodded sideways, thick tresses tumbling around her shoulders and pulsing down her back. It was quite a change from the high bun she wore at work with tendrils framing her beautiful round face. Through the dining room was a ten-foot by ten-foot sunroom with glass walls. The sun streamed in, illuminating the room like a prism of light. Rashad, Brianna, and all the guests were happy as hot, sweaty, naked mole rats cuddling against each other.

"What's happening?" Akar asked in wonder.

"It happens every time I have people over. They all crowd in there." Chantelle cocked her head. In a dreamy voice she mused, "That's my meditation room. I pray in there twice a day. When I walk in there, I immediately feel God's presence. They might not recognize what it is, but maybe on some level, they feel it too."

The Takeaway

Mindfulness didn't make the CEO of Akar's company nicer. Nor did it cure Chantelle's husband's post-traumatic stress disorder caused by his military experiences. It wasn't a miracle cure, but their God-centered meditation practice did allow Akar and Chantelle to weather challenges with much greater equanimity. God poured into them clarity of purpose, peace, love, and joy. It can do the same for you. Stay on your mindfulness journey. It will bring you greater peace.

WHERE YOU GO FROM HERE

Congratulations for completing *Mindful in 5, God Lovers' Edition!* Consider revisiting chapters that challenged you. Some might take years to master, and that's perfectly all right because mindfulness is a journey, not a destination. Use this book as a reference tool to support you along your way.

If you haven't already, I invite you to open your heart and invite God into your life. Embrace His love, forgiveness, and transformative power. It is never too late to turn from our wrong ways of living and choose a path of righteousness guided by His wisdom and grace. Let go of the burdens that weigh you down and find solace in His presence. Allow Him to heal your wounds, restore your soul, and lead you to a life filled with purpose and joy. May you experience the freedom and peace that come from surrendering to God's loving embrace. Embrace this invitation and embark on a journey of transformation, knowing that God's abundant grace awaits you. How do you do that? You can recite a prayer of invitation, such as:

Dear God,

I open my heart to invite You into my life. I embrace Your love, forgiveness, and transformative power. I am sorry for all the wrong I have thought and done. Today, I choose to turn from my wrong ways of living and follow Your path of righteousness. I release the burdens that weigh me down and find solace in Your presence. Heal my wounds, restore my soul, and guide me to a life filled with purpose and joy. I surrender to Your loving embrace, experiencing the freedom and peace that come from walking with You. Thank You for Your abundant grace. Amen.

If you enjoyed taking this journey, please leave a review at Amazon.com or Goodreads.com. Subscribe to and rate the *Mindful in 5* podcast on your favorite podcast platform. Use the QR code below to visit the website and download sample chapters for upcoming books, watch videos, check out podcast episodes, and sign up for companion emails, and insider notices for upcoming books and events.

Pick up the other books in this series, including the first book: *Mindful in 5 – Meditations for People With No Time,* and the companion *Mindful in 5 Journal.* Also look for future books in the series, including the next book, *Mindful in 5 for Perpetual Optimists.*

Now that you have tools to increase inner happiness starting with just five minutes a day, I sincerely hope you enjoy the benefits and harness the power of mindfulness to operate from your peaceful path, and live and work to your highest and best purpose each day. May God bless you in your every endeavor. Be mindful and be well.

Printed in the United States
by Baker & Taylor Publisher Services